I0623670

Published by Authors Branding
9620 Las Vegas Blvd S Ste E4 632
Las Vegas, NV 89123, USA
support@authorsbranding.com
(725) 240-6558

ISBN: 979-8-9908049-7-5 (paperback)
ISBN: 979-8-9908049-8-2 (ebook)

# TABLE OF CONTENTS

# OCTOBER BLUE

SHAWAYNE DUNSTAN

# October Blue

## Shawayne Dunstan

*I did the best I could and I came as far as I should...*

Shawayne Dunstan's view of the world is like a fine art piece that keeps you engaged the longer you look at it. He takes words which you or me use each day and delivers a skin tingling sensation that encourages you to look deeper within. He overcomes all obstacles with such grace and resilience and I feel confident in allowing him to share his views unhinged. Whether it was choosing the correct format or wording of his poems to the challenges that arises with production companies, Shawayne never failed at making sure the his books were a perfect rendition of his feelings. I am proud to be apart of his journey, I am overjoyed to have been able to experience each book, each progression, each celebration with my brother Shawayne. I love the way his mind works and I love him. Thank you for allowing me to be apart of book 10 and in his words "It's a good day to have a great day".

—Kimone Dunstan

# INTRODUCTION

A reflection on perception
I worry just the same
If you lacked any direction
Here be another poem by Shawayne

Exploration of the mind
Closure for the heart
In this context I unwind
In the public eye I climb charts

The ego is tame
Beauty found within
We trade our pain
I need you to win

#10 in the series
#1 in your heart
In case you're still curious
Allow me to simply start

# List of Books Authored
# by Shawayne Dunstan

- GUILTY BY ASSOCIATION
- THE UNDISPUTED DEFEAT OF AN ADOLESCENT
- WALLFLOWER
- LOOSE CHANGE AND PINEAPPLE WAVES
- POOR MAN'S NECTAR
- THE UNDISPUTED DEFEAT OF AN ADOLESCENT REMASTERED
- DRUNKEN FIREFLIES FROM SOMBER LULLABIES
- THIS SHARED MOMENT WITH YOU
- TUMBLEBUG
- OCTOBER BLUE

*Shaweezy Publications*

The Journey? If you asked me what I thought about Shawayne when I met him in high school I'd tell you the same thing now; he's destined for GREATNESS. He's never failed to impress, his accomplishments? I promise you those were set in stone especially when Shaweezy was born in civics & careers class. From reading his work in the middle of class to speaking at school assembly meetings to becoming our valedictorian and publishing in 2016 while still in high school and now seeing him publishing book #10 is the greatness I'm talking about. The number 10 is an important number that not only represents beginnings but also endings. Shawayne's journey to book #10 'October Blue' is his deep breath into a new beginning to his journey to greatness but also a deep breath out of his old one. The journey is the destination but the destination would be nothing without the journey. Regardless of where he is or where he ends up I hope you know Shawayne Dunstan is nothing short of GREAT.

I hope you always remember that Shawayne. I carry a lot of respect and love for you always!

—Keya <3

Without further ado, Welcome to October Blue!

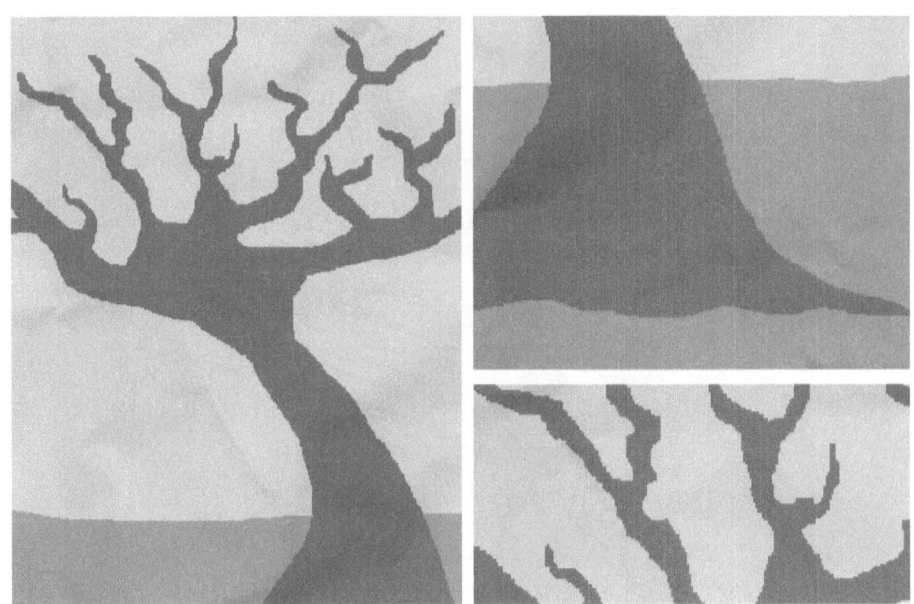

# AFTER GLOW

"The world cannot be changed with view skewed.
May we heal from pain and put a cease to feuds."

Shawayne D                    June 4 2024

# SILVER LINING IN PERPLEXITY

Allow me to shower you with roses
On the eve of eclipses imminent
The guilt that you've been holding
Provokes the question if we're even friends

I want you to holster the confusion
Breathe in the hope invoked by birds that sing
I live my life by simply cruising
But what of potholes that indecision brings?

Self-expression be the weapon worthy
I know I bleed the blood of '99
Even if you continue to disagree
Pretentious figures drinking wine

Strung around fingers like cotton candy
The proof is found in the dough
Abundance appeared is absolutely filthy
Self-actualization is the balance you owe

# PAIN IN YOUR EYES

I look within
Eyes that aren't mine
We met on a whim
You were the shy porcupine

No need for glasses testing
I see signs that divinity sent
No need for outrageous flexing
Beauty beneath the cement

World view and hope illuminated
I reckon we've got a bit of time
I fell in love with you during conversation
Growth was taught to this heart of mine

Speak not on the shame
We only hold understanding here
In your eyes I saw pain
And in that moment I wanted to disappear

I see your face in dreams
Provoked by this dysfunctional imagination
I am truly not whom I seem
But I know the ambition is not a limitation

# Cloud is Insomnia

I float
With no destination in mind
Mercy me so
I wish to be here in the summertime

God willing
I turn mistakes into lessons
Truth revealing
I should take pride in my complexion

Path unpaved
Undertaken off a fluke
Save me the day
At night, my demons gather in groups

I am divine interference
Closure to the affluent soul
Step into the light rather than fear it
Come inside little one, outside is cold

Generational pain
Nipped at the roots
If there be violence unchanged
I will pray that they don't shoot

# Déjà Vu

Gates of opportunity
Reluctance to calmly speak
For the sake of sanity
Make sure you wash your feet

I'm not sure the way
So why you listening still?
A lie of being okay
But the soul refused to be killed

I plead my case
Of subtlety overlooked
The destruction I create
Was ignited by the first book

If this be truth laced
I trip with intolerance to enlightenment
If bitterness we taste
We are victims to the perpetual violence

Voice is a stranger to the stage
I fear this is no time to be cowardice
They stole the words from my page
Good thing I topped my old shit

# GUIDE TO NOWHERE

Pink grapefruit
Cotton candy sky
Uphold your roots
Quotes we live by

Finding peace within
I'm no stranger to hurt
In you I begin
Rumination works

Bond broken
Or so it seems
Light mustn't dim
Freedom is longevity

What's craved in-between
Birth and death?
If vulnerability is on scene
This is a chapter I reflect

The cherry was admired
Appearances can deceive
Sour taste discovered
Excommunicated by the seed

# LIME GREEN EPIPHANIES

Why shy away from restitution?
Taking of a value was their contribution

I'm using words sleek in the spring heat
Sun has me weak, limited by ability to speak

And elaborate of the view to our world divine
Be not still beam with your essence prime

I'm the shy porcupine to the pessimistic fox
Even when the world treats you unkind

I love you lots, words I jot to address vices
Chance are you spot victim to the dices

Ignorance is bliss and camaraderie sweet
Broken down ablaze, lime green epiphanies

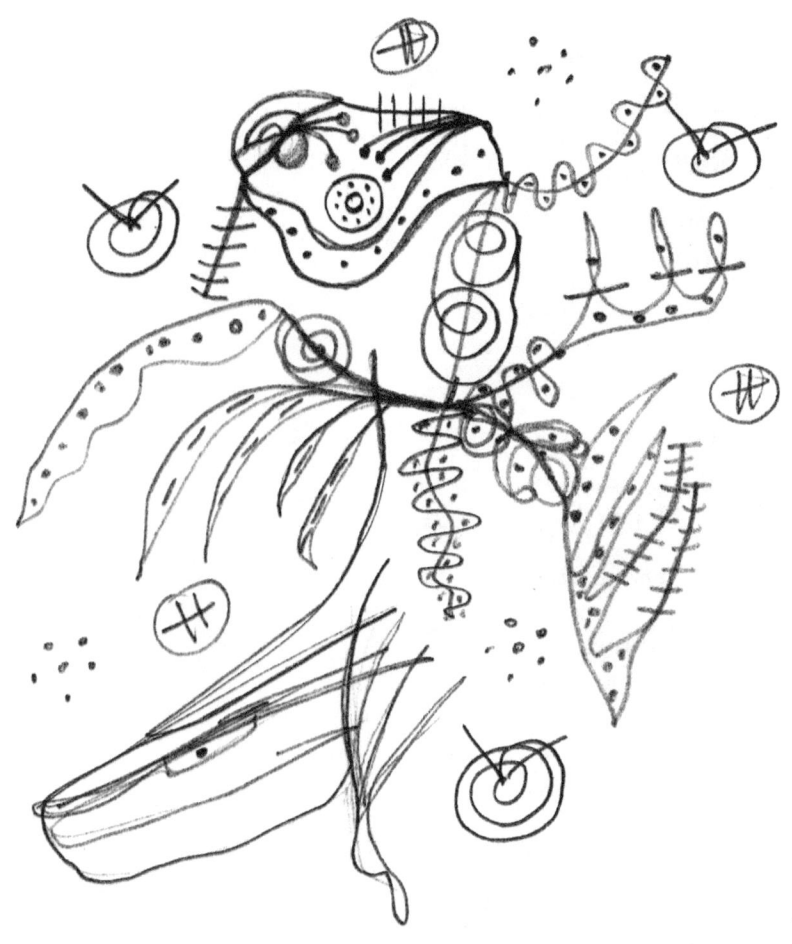

NShawayneD                    June 4 2024

# SMOKEY HUE, BORN ANEW

I need to focus more
Find power in my core
Find a reason to live for
While navigating rich and poor

Needs and wants
You are truth I see
Falsity pleads inherently
Vulnerability I shouldn't see

Perfection overrated on a daily
Diving in with no parachute for safety
Wake me please, but into me breathe
Philosophy of seed blooming into trees

Blue skies all around
Cotton candy clouds
Peace of mind found
Company with no sound

Rose kissed mountaintops
Represent how I love you lots
The world is full of so many nots
Pursuing the good is your best shot

# BRETHREN, REVERENDS AND COFFINS

Tried to tell them about divine interference
But the truth was they didn't want to hear it
I felt the envy and greed seeping endlessly
It wasn't up to fate rather destiny

To not be caught lacking
Plotting when we were laughing
Gunshot into stained tees
Tears of you without me

This be poetry in motion
I'm Shaweezy with ill methods of coping
What is spoken be plans to speed demise
I'm just hoping you have heart to look into eyes

I and I as you are you
Black or white, red or blue
Sanity abused when I overthink
But that could've been my blood in the sink

Hugs exchanged, cashmere suits in the rain
Monetary gain, but karma plays a funny game

# MILKY WAY

This isn't a poem about being okay
Rather alone and afraid
Of what the mind might do
Stress induced visions abused

Why are they leaving again?
Just to pop up when I'm making friends
Shadows creeping to tarnish a period of peace
Tears seeping as I say to you why I feel weak

In this world of ours
My heart I guard
On starry May nights
Is it discontent you see in eyes?

Mission to do more than settle
Lonesome days I feel like a vegetable
I can not save nor be like you
I'd be amazed if this be a long-life cycle

# *If There Be Turquoise, Proceed*

I'm a mess, filled with stress
Body wrecked, hands caress
With intentions of safety, no maybes
Confirmation lately, I've been suffering greatly

Subtle cracks in facade, against odds
All the head bops, certified heart throb
Isn't life about growth, rejuvenated hope
When you spoke, disengaged on somber notes

Opposite of hibernation, overdue patience
Never mind conversation, focus on destination
Swim not drown my friend, content in the end
Woes pitted against, purified from offence

I shy away discreetly, unworthy of matrimony
Water set you free, baptism to a lesser degree

# Momma Cloak

Who am I kidding?
Can't really express the feeling
Of generational hurt passed down
To my children

Lessons into mistakes be hitting
I'm not virtuous like you—
To leave
Unannounced

I struggle to breathe
In the absence of doubt
That we could work things out
Maybe I would have chosen a different route

But isn't this what's been given
Through transgressions and spillage
Of blood, tears and sweat
Your cloak didn't really intercept

Rather kept watch as I sidestepped death
Time after time
You are the flitting thought combined
With misery's sins

How can you so easily dance in the wind?

# SHUN ME NOT, I HEAL TOO

I'm a visionary in a dystopian era
Mixing vices and temporary pleasure
I could never love you better anyway
The fact I'm feeling off-centred illuminates

My place in the human race, thriving
With steady pace, unlearned is to wait
Moreover or less you get what you get
This ability to create bringing in the checks

Focus on your breath amid ego death
Flame introduced to moth, cold winds blew
Shun me not, I heal too
Sometimes

Eventually
When I get lost in my mind
I remember what you meant to me
Breathe I said, ever so long and deep
Wedding bells...I'm not the one doing a speech

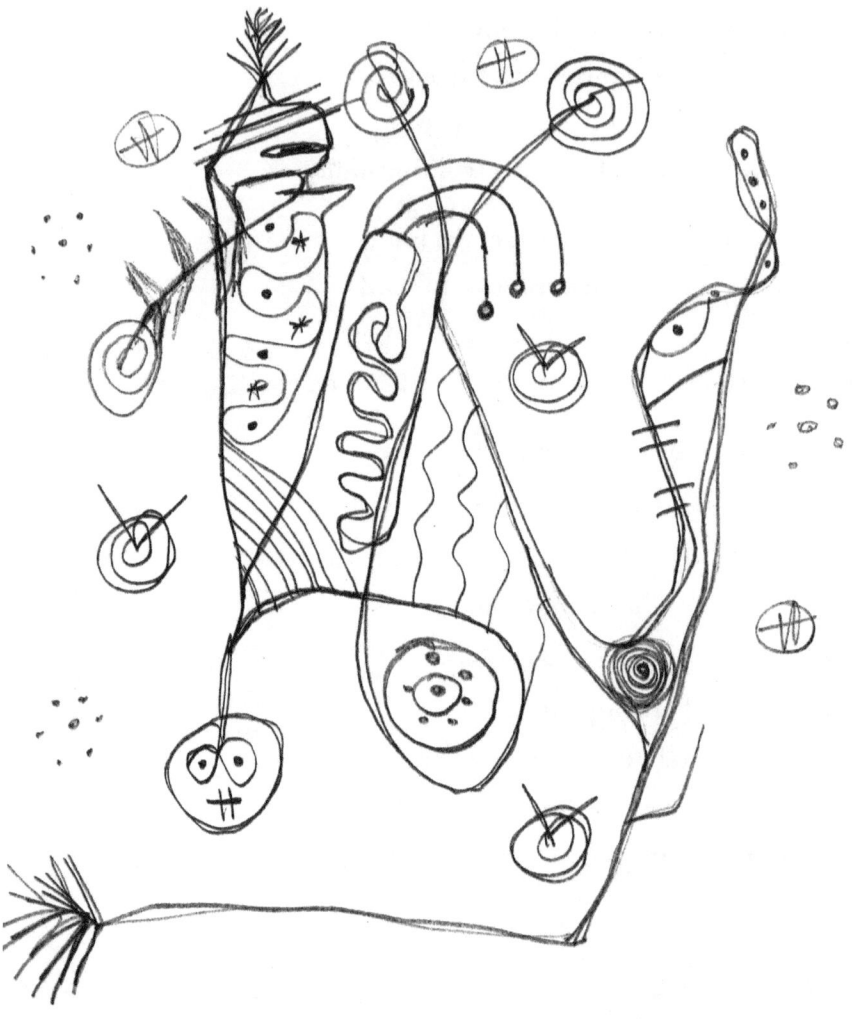

NBharaynel)                              June 4 2024

# BREAD AND BUTTER

This whole daily struggle thing ain't working
I need confirmation after I've atoned for sins
I need gold to lace the words from my mouth
And you fall in love with them without a doubt

Depressed infiltrated unprovoked
Ill methods to cope when I lost hope
Jah guidance went unheard despite cries
Human like you, exemplified by tears in eyes

I see crusades from a refuge of safety
Why must I care if they love or hate me?
Especially when bitterness is potent in hearts
They're hurting too, I saw the blood and scars

Fundamentally stricken with ancestral trauma
Creativity bestowed from lessons in drama
The day belongs to you and blue skies
I see cloudy hues and vengeful apartheid

# PRODIGY IN SUMMER HEAT

So here we go
Into mind that reaps
What is sowed
Blistering hope

Reimagined in smoke
I see this as a joke...
If there be painful interval
I sidestep like potholes

Anxiety is the fuel
What is chicken to road?
Sympathy unrecognized
When I spot tears from eyes

I have internalized
I'm the bad guy
Wither me with generosity
Therapy without animosity

Agree to disagree, we are free
To be whoever we'd like to be

# WICKEDLY DONE, DON'T RUN

I rose this morning with intention
The rain falling I don't need to mention
Persevered through with errands to uphold
If I'm being true, I'm haunted by visions of soul

I suppose ten toes deep in concrete
My will still weak and talk is ever so cheap
This be Shaweezy taking it easy with the flow
The world needs me, but right now I don't owe

Explanation illuminated in the heart
Pain able to break rumination from the start
If we're apart I'm a figment of your imagination
When it gets dark, allow joy into conversation

No cotton candy skies or tender hues
Only jealousy resides as they aim at you
Ain't no coming back from this hun
Although wickedly done, don't run

# DIVINE INTERCEPTION, UNLOVABLE AGGRESSION

Reflecting in the hollows of destitution
Pardon me for the delay in fruition
Of one of my greatest works
I deserve recognition for my hurt

Nothing less than direct when I accept
Not settling for less, I'm out of breath—
Poor me oh my with hands to the sky
Wishful thinking gets me institutionalized

Find me afar, but close just the same
Look at the stars and you'll glimpse my pain
Affluent in reasons to wreck havoc evermore
Insomnia's cloud is a hammock, life is a chore

Of tasks and moments tender sweet
Your power of change is how you speak
Knowledge paves the way, ill-hearts rejoice
If we so casually lay, enrich me with your voice

# LONGEST HUG TREASURED, GONE FOREVER UNTIL TIMES BETTER

I tried to pull away, but you were holding on
Type of love that can't be conveyed by poem
I wrote a song then crumpled the pages
Forgive me for wrongs like untied shoelaces

Can't be blamed when fate takes the wheel
Why am I feeling drained, this is a time to heal
Everything is nothing in this place of sublime
Yet I hold you to something mindful and divine

Maybe you'll see through cracks in the ego
How must I not provoke with words I wrote?
Missing is only an intermission
Set mind to task at hand for a difference

I can't begin to speak these months pure
I'm left in awe after being absolutely unsure
You feel like home unbounded and hope anew
Even if I'm left alone I know I can't covet you

# I'M REALLY HIM

Awaiting the arrival of the next generation
Continuous cycle where we avoid conversation
The last relation severed due to ambition
For you to stay is the only thing I'm wishing

Mystery surrounding what's come and went
I tried to explain, but didn't make sense
Like the rose that evaded the cement
Will you hear me true if I chase sentiments

Through these words in this moment
The person in the mirror is my only opponent
Rising me with promises of prevalence
Tearing me down with unmindful comments

I've got gratitude spilling over double time
But the issues fizzle with claims I'm fine
I once wrote about the cost of a dime
Would it provoke if I didn't finish the last—

Shawn D                                    June 4 2024

# JUSTIFICATION

Rubber bands and ink stains
Y'all tried to warn me about the fame
"There is beauty in elusiveness Shawayne..."

I need them to feel my pain and presence
Liable to cover the world with my essence
The fact that I ain't bullet proof is reflected

In poems that don't stretch out to you
Blacken toes despite steel boots
I'm at war with my inner attributes

But I want y'all to simply succeed
A brother from Malton with justification of we
Power indeed no matter colour nor creed

Who are you not to be great?
Absolute shame if you settled for last place
Calculating the next step as you flip life's page

The craze of it all will leave you dismantled
Regardless growth is something you'll handle
With the power you have to be responsible

I still see your pain
— A poet named Shawayne

# Know Not What I Knew

And something seems like it's still missing
Recognition I'm getting yet feeling indifferent
What happened to the consistency unswayed?
My first mistake was asking if you were okay

Could I handle the weight of vulnerability?
Upmost highs tangled with inevitable lows
Fears speak to me as I'm muted by society
Unfamiliarity sowed invokes me staying 10toes

Deep in cement, regressions haunt a minor me
I bet you'd take all the precautions and such
Even if you disagree, the budget prompts envy
Ask too much, is your soul bankrupt?

Done with ease, the summer brings us closer
Comprehensive of divinity and soulful words
May what you search for enable you closure
Imagine if I wrote all of this poem backwards?

# XUMI

Wash me with your generational power
Spinning the sun, this may be the final hour
I second the thought when I think of what's lost
Ambition is the cost, are you the runoff?

Absolute devotion as we step into the open
I've grown since our last moment spoken
Behind the scenes, hopes to intervene
My ego is weak, I cannot scream mercy

Hurt me with truth of dissatisfaction
I plant roots in the field of love everlasting
Not the norm for me to speak on the urge
I weather your storm hoping to purge

# 2 IN THE AM

Thoughts invade when the mind is led astray
How I allow them to talk to me that way?
Where I'm from that ain't no easy feat
To sit back, let shit slide while grinding my teeth

I'm an optimist most days let alone some
Don't want to pry, but curious who hurt you hun
I should resort to violence and exaggeration
Healing should be the topic of conversation

Putting my best foot forward everyday
Yet you always find negativity to convey
I don't give a damn how your life is tough
We all trying to make it out the rough

Swallow the ego and digest it slow
We're empowered with the more we know
Maybe what you went through was terrible
Ain't no excuse for you being fucking miserable

# SILVERSTONE DRIVE

Expression to my seed that I need healing
Truth revealing that I can be deceiving
I pray for better before their arrival
Concrete jungle as I sidestep idols

Stuck on a pivot, I succumb to the dark
Blood is residual, dagger in your heart
How much it cost for you to slow down
World turned around, ain't no reason to frown

Procrastination invades during my element
Everyone gets paid including the government
Writers block still ain't no excuse for time delay
Why are you willing to shoot if I choose to stay

I need island sun and coconut rum
I need to undertake the person I'll become
It ain't easy, but apparently written in the sand
Shocked at the world's cruelty, please take my hand...

# AT MY TABLE

Brothers through thick and thin
Women who want to see me win
Individuals with no underlying motives
People that can look in my eyes when toasting

Whole devotion to the common good
If there be commotion, you've misunderstood
Over here we despise fear and early demise
All that boasting can't ease tears amid lies

I'll be alright as we feast and joke
Summer heat, circle of flavourful smoke
I've awoken to abundance and reparations
Might not make sense yet life lies in patience

Hold the conversation of dreams with us
It's alright, this is a representation of my trust
I heard a hungry mind leads to a lonely soul
So come on let's eat before the food gets cold

r8hawayneD                    June 5 2024

# GRATIFICATION FROM DISCOMFORT

It's a nasty feeling
Staring at the ceiling
With tears seeping
Into sheets

That gossip about me
When I'm not around
Homie said stay ten toes down
In this concrete jungle

"My brother, we love you"
Ain't no better thing to do
That arise with my head high
Truth revealed that maybe I don't want to fly

Course corrected from choosing to die here
"If that be confession, don't succumb to fear"
It is what it is, I need to live it out
Going along the unpaved route

The sedatives and vices won't always work
Discomfort known since overdue birth

# SATURATED FLORENCE

I can't speak on the ill moments
Abundance wrapped in philanthropy
Life is bonus, do I deserve consistency?

To some degree my woes hath no notion
Come with me across the ocean waves
Alkaline vibes while we steady the motion

This is me persevering as birds chirp
Legendary core, I give thanks for those before
Generational person, I see myself in your hurt

# ASTRONOMICAL LIGHT, I SACRIFICE SIGHT

How must I convey galactic mercy
To bring forth this person before me
I held the faith to a lesser degree
Mindful obligations disregard lack of maturity

With eyes front and centre I proceed
Tree of life reveals the worthy seed
You deserve to be acknowledged and freed
I'm not the hero nor the saviour you need

Anxiety invades on lonesome days
Yet chosen was the unpaved way
Intention to shelter me and say, "It's okay"
I should mention darkness is what I undertake

Heartache soothed, in the middle rooted
With dedication to reaffirm when I lose it
Proof in the aura, but time frame tragic
"I'm forever here for you in the spirit"

# PICK A STRUGGLE

No dependency when ego is matured bless
Sadness takes residency wherein I cry less
Upside down, right side up, matrix interferes
I dawn a frown, pain struck, changing gear

Silent prayer to higher power and younger me
I'm a fighter, but right now I'm tired recklessly
Gifted hearts lifted with words tenderly cold
I believe in people, and I believe in the soul

What a cycle of events and things amuck
I was prideful during the journey of the book
Never imagined I could describe my routine
I feel weary, hopeful and capable of means

Clawed my way from cement, made sense
For there now there is now, dreams and rent
Invisible made clear to eyes closed suddenly
The afterglow emerges from darkness weak

With that the year weans and unwinds
It's rather immaculate to feel sunshine
I don't know if it will be okay tomorrow
Maybe another day is how we pay sorrow

# DESERT STORM

My older sister proud
Embrace me with passion loud
I still believe in all the people
Shelter not with the words lethal

I'm still numbing the pain
Thinking of trauma sustained
Better must come I reckon
Not a guarantee rather a reflection

Human as best discovered
Faith reinforced when I stuttered
Out the gutter and on to something new
In your desert storm I see mirages blue

Pour me one with no repercussions
Healing should be topic of discussion
Never fronting when I say I pain deeply
Didn't expect to get this far in society

Little do they know; you reap what you sow
Livid ego means collars soaked and provoked
I fear our hope is snuffed by ceilings dire
My older sister proud of soul unfit to tire

# Apple Juice

Conversations from way back then
Re-emerge ever so potent once again
I choose to dive and plant some roots
You are the cup to my chilled apple juice

I think about of you now and then
We aren't acquaintances nor friends
I reckon you still got all those dreams
Haven't seen you in the flesh yet I fiend

Proclamations of the lonesome side
I put in the work with no tears in eyes
Sacrificial means in which I advise hope
Collar unclean, may I take time to cope?

Hero without cape, I people please daily
Harnessed the mentality nobody will save me
Battered hands so I pause to admire view
You are the cup to my chilled apple juice

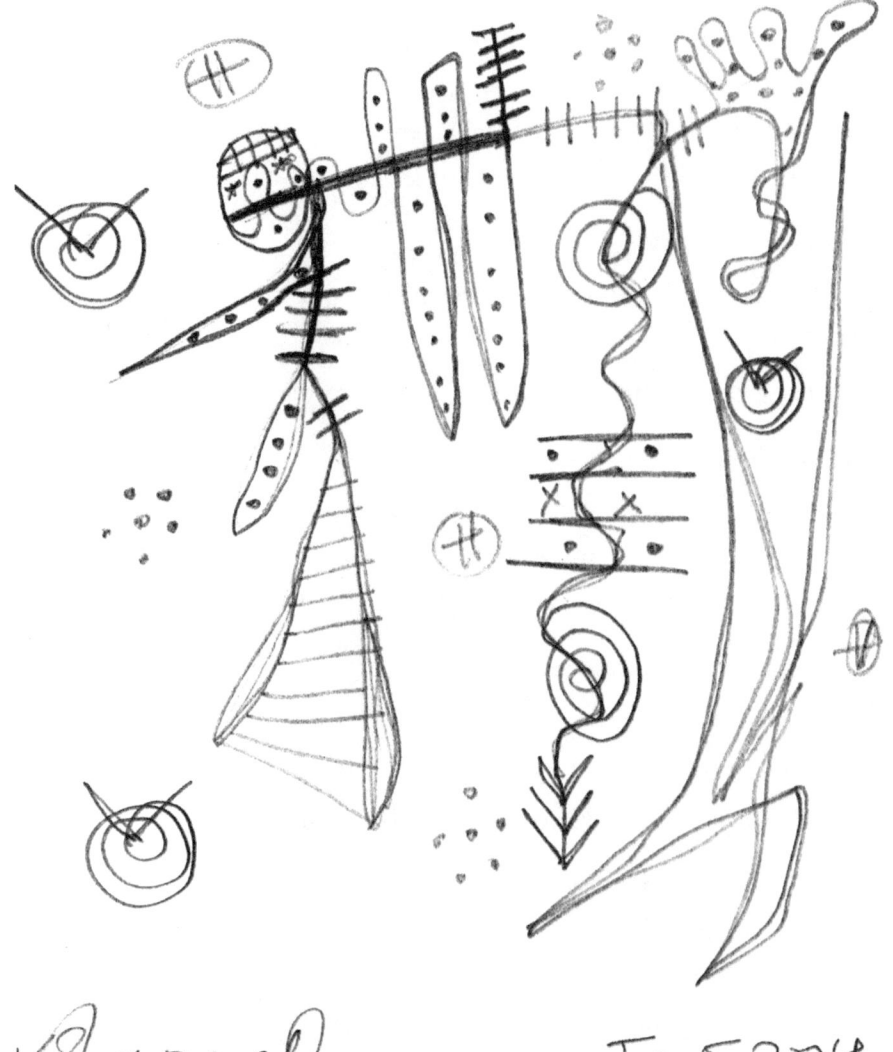

Shawrynel                    June 5 2024

# HALLELUJAH

Melodic blue in passionate hue
I wish to give more, but I have coins few
The fortunate truth is that I pain too
Elaboration while breaking down before you

Is the good enough for my safe keeping
I know their ultimatums are dire and whatnot
Is it still love although she's not speaking
Tears on sleeves and clutched fists are tragic

I bite my tongue cause ego will win
What plans have you lain out before my soul
I am not perfect for I have already sinned
Heard to soothe the heart that's grown cold

Like the air I need and the water too
This is lived experience of giving hope a try
You cannot pour from empty bucket, true
However rejuvenating is the past getting by

I say a prayer and analyze time on clock
Crystallized rain drops flinch at umbrella
This is not a marathon, but a stride full walk
A moment I was lost then found, hallelujah

# 2:30

Hair still nappy like dreadlock
Words I jot for their head top
Passionately slow with no liquor to pour
Blessed a couple years, here's to some more

Walking down Keele, not a dream, this real
I've been cursed to feel, seems ideal to deal
Giving heart cause I spotted you in the dark
Emotions parked at the most lonesome mark

Do you feel the same way when spoken is pain
Energetic to drained is the core of the game
What don't I deserve when abundance I seek
Freedom from misery into overwhelming greed

Internalization that I can be the reason you cry
Sunrise on the go train, no destination so I sigh
Weight evermore lessened; another year gifted
Alpha 82, modern struggle, may God be lifted

# ISET

Life be lifing, but I love all the people
We be trying despite bullets that are lethal
Good ones go into the night like stars so bright
My appetite is for reparations from sacrifice

Momma Africa, I pray for all my sisters
Well wishes to save them from the sinners
I ain't holy nor pardoned from dismal cause
But if you truly know me, you'd say love is law

In my hands are stones from Zion
The land is home, yet I owe someone
Disrespect is fuel for composure provoked
Drowning in debt for they dashed the rope

Hello future self with abundance of wealth
I carry desolation shouldered by cards dealt
Words suitable to comfort in January's hue
Life be lifing and I love all the people like you

# Drown the Drip

White picket fence to establish status
They're friends yet hidden within is malice
I pardon the fears of my younger self
Commitment is near for I choose no-one else

I've been hurting yet I choose to emerge again
Alice in Wonderland, feed them cake in the end
A piece of me in exchange for understanding
Eulogy written to the fear what future will bring

Pardon my sins and dire attitude
I need to win therefore I can't rock with you
Still no saint or saviour in the slightest
Monarchs faint at star shining brightest

Shelter me and the lonely heart
You may drown the drip, but beware the heart
Of poet with scars uncounted and smile
The demons once mounted after utter denial

# NOSTALGIC DIARY

Still with the dream
Affirmations seen
The need to persevere
Please hold loved ones near

Can't lie about challenges less
The horizon holds pain and stress
Won't sugarcoat like most do
This life will utterly shape you

Break you to the tune of interlude passionate
That's misguidance and angst on their breath
Walk into the night with future bright
It's perfectly alright that's not your life

Nostalgic diary filled with confessions potent
You making out the concrete makes sense
I need to provide more, creating a ripple effect
I need to give all I can afford, lean from death

I need to finish this poem, it's time to sleep
I need to nourish the body, take time to eat
I need to listen with no interruptions
I need to show my pain with no bluffing

I need to finish this and sign the bottom
I need to made a wish without divine mocking

# GLENDAVUDE

With an earnest heart I say
Peace of mind brought on today
With your perfect sway and remarks
Shelter me whole and lead me through dark

Not as lyrical yet still affectionate
I'm spiritual when it comes to making a wish
To see you in good health and in love with self
Change starts when cold heart gleefully melts

I'm jotting this with the end in mind
Heads bopping as I drink fortified wine
Does it get better than this which I see?
No Kendrick to guide butterfly from concrete

You're perfect, you're true, I'm in love with you
No sense, pain overdue, I need to heal too
I cover my scars with dollar bills and poetry
Suffering tremendously, a mill is what I need

The money eventually dries up
I grow numb to your touch
The body is constantly starving
You represent Mars and I'm a lost Martian

shawayneD                    June 7 2024

# WINDMILL

Sunny daze
Lonesome ways
Cookie crumbles
Everybody paid

Beyond recognition
Something is missing
Brutal honesty incurs
Should've left the kitchen

Haters gonna hate
Can't be late today
Showing up for myself
I try to keep the faith

Sporadic missions
Coincidental competition
I fear what I don't know
Can't settle for submission

Round and round
I rise from off the ground
Mounted the train of grief
Windmill mocking in the east

# I NEVER COULD, I NEVER WOULD

Brush my shoulders off
The battle ain't close to done
Opponents continue to scoff
I find power without a gun

Complexion relevant amid turmoil
Black history evident every single day
Compulsive narrative over boulders
I deserve to achieve everything I say

Never wanted to bring pain
But capable none the less
I've been feeling quite strange
I find peace amid the stress

Worthy of walking into the night
You've got a family too I bet
I'm a pacifist so I don't fight
You're an academic with hatred on breath

Chance after chance
I'll leave the rest for you to discover
I don't got time to dance
Crimson rain drenching the cupboards

# MACHIAVELLI ENTOURAGE

Analyzation of prior work through the years
You're looking for a response so this is it here
I spew these words vicious despite pleas true
I don't got time to say I care rather fuck you

I'm sane in the head till the moment I'm not
I was about to disengage, but you talk a lot
Didn't follow dreams and now fiending as I jot
Looking to tear me down with ruthless plots

My brother, you try to be him, but you're not
Rather than hold a conversation, you stalk
Life sad, money never had, and women resent
Poetry in motion as I say you're a fraud to men

I'm pissed, rightfully so, you make me sick
Fake jewellery on wrist, lost hope, severed bliss
I don't care yet I take time to drive this deep
I'm a pacifist, but you...are a novice to streets

Weight of my name gathers storms of crowds
Never liked you then and it's still disgust now
I should flow better to satisfy the whole world
Open letter, jig is up, she's an independent girl

# PARTNERS IN TIME

You don't need saving
I'm still healing slow
The need for elevation
Frees us from the smoke

Hope not guaranteed
Be with me for now
If along comes a seed
I'll surely water the ground

Could this be the embodiment
Of destination and self actualization
I'm told that we're built different
Yet my future detests stagnation

Like the moth to a flame
Like the ocean to the moon
Partner without name
I wish to see you soon

# TOTALITY

Your memory exists yet it is something
That won't be missed in the morning
I solidify the art of getting by
Routine being a vice and arms to the sky

The noise and drama are unsettling
Not listening so asked what change you bring
Desolation softly, scars reek of hunger
My vocation is calling from depths of October

Garments, windows and scripture
Not in the physical yet we still feel hurt
Outside reminiscent of peace capable
Please share your voice if you're able

I say a silent prayer in the midst of celebration
In the totality of life, please value patience

# WITH YOU HERE NOW

The point is to heal
But I matured numb
Figments weren't real
My whole identity spun

I meant to cry, storm beloved
There's a deeper issue at hand
Compassion is part of the budget
Words as the tool rather weapons

The distance is an issue
I'm healing ever so slow
If your shadow bit you
Would you even know?

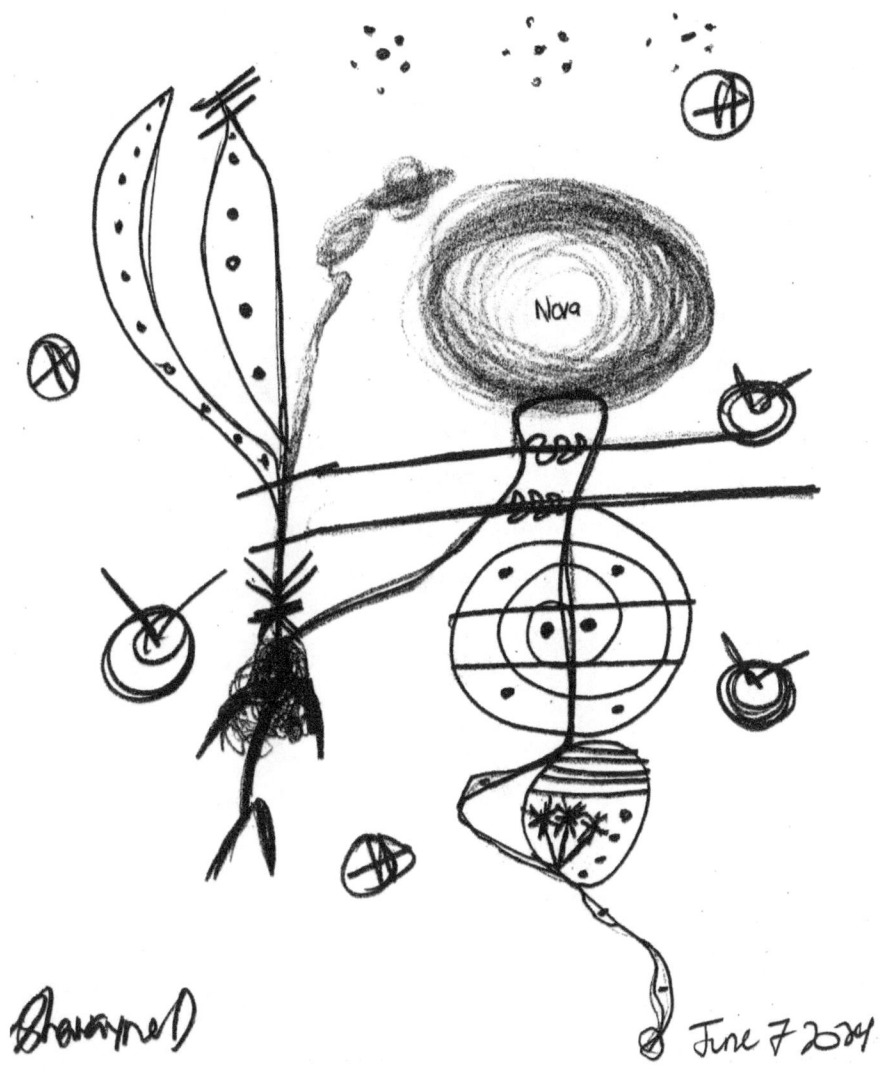

Nova

Shaunne)     June 7 2024

# ADJACENT

Left the door to my mind slightly ajar
In reality I have come quite very far
I should know better, this world being cold
With this stormy weather, just need one to hold

Still don't got all the answers to tribulations
Pain I see in humanity initiates conversations
Voice is breaking as I elude to all the fear
Bursting at the seams, but all you do is stare

On this side, realization that I wasn't ready
On that side, perceived as the body of enemy
Within, I tell the cells emancipation will come
Outside, the joke is me choosing to run

# ROAD TEST

Never mind what's better
Never mind what's worst
As you secure all the gains
May your dreams not get murked

I can not claim you
This is a soulful interlude
Prior to eulogy and fame
I will try to pray for you

Glorious life and passion
Give onto him with no asking
Perhaps heart is pure from start
May you finally begin unmasking

This is a family matter
This one for moments of laughter
Problems, we all got them
I hope to see you after stormy weather

Righteous as the sun
Close as the moon
Awesome as a possum
Please come home soon

# SLIGHT OF HAND

All at stake
All for grabs
Life I've had
You say don't be sad

Tattered cape
Mirrored stagnation
Potent observation
Actions don't need justification

I yearn your faith
Visions became blurred
My stomach just surged
Disgusted with cold words

What's a rope to a lake
Simple means blunt
Captivation is a front
In the back counting ones

No need to procrastinate
I felt the hate in a dark room
The cloud was irritated as it loomed
I aimed for stars cause I couldn't see the moon

# IMMACULATE

"I hope it all works out in the grand scheme of things. Right now we're good, but I'm excited for what future may bring."

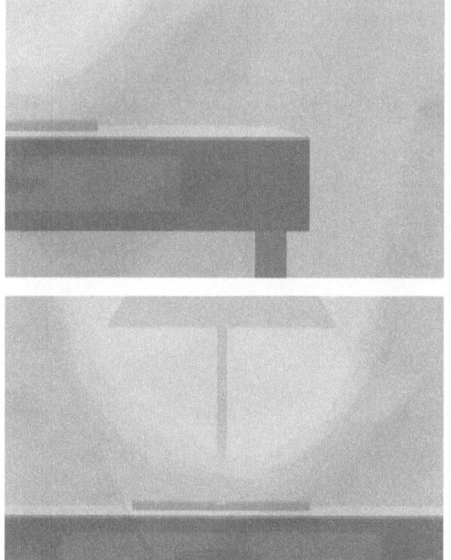

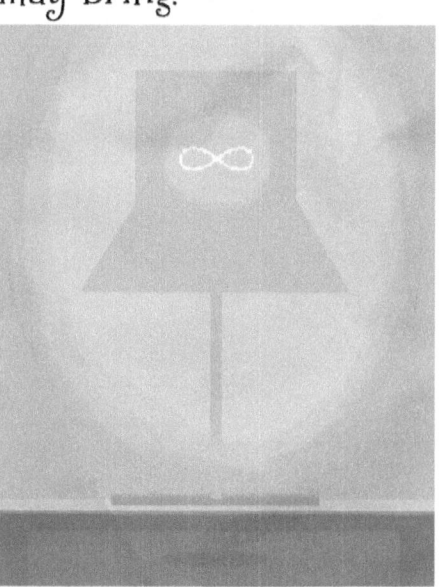

# KEYA

2016 seems like a lifetime ago
I say what I mean, heart melts with the snow
Profound resonance with affirmations
I'd like to thank you for teaching me patience

Long before Shaweezy manifested
You enforced that I was course corrected
To something better than the inevitable norm
I can imagine how the distance left you torn

But you wanted me to soar new heights
Being on a pedestal brought me fright
Lesson that I had to fight and scream
In your eyes, a true poet I was deemed

Never anticipated to make it this far
All those moments I was told I'd be a star
Million-dollar dreams yet bitterness known
Day 1 supporter, I think you deserve the throne

# In Lieu Of The New

Same problems and pitfalls
Rip-offs with direct insults
Mood solemn and cigars menthol
Depression smirks at withdrawal

It may hurt, but guilt lurks
Gratitude with no perks
Could be absolutely worst
Public feuds with no search

Malibu on a summer night
Waking up spoils the sight
Drawing strength from the sun's light
Maybe today everything will be alright

Expect the same and never worry
For when it rains I am sorry
Being one with nature was your story
I refrain from melancholic purgatory

Shawyne D      June 23 2024

# PLEASE COME BACK, DON'T COME BACK

Outwards I stretch
But your avoidance reeks
Immaturity unrefined
I care not
Less than prior

To coming to my senses
I breathe magentas
I speak passion
I weep destitution

Rhyme or reason other
I choose not to bother
I remain mute at the alter

# AT LEAST ONE OF US IS ALONE

I told you that the words were the sword
Can I get my flowers before casket is lowered?
Destined for more than a fateful end
King of wagons, but I'm a mortal man

I mourn the tune of Sunday morning
Rain outside pouring, but far from boring
Mellow like jello I whisper to my shadow
Star struck at hello, I'm a gentle fellow

Precious mind deconstructing euphoria divine
You taste like wine and look like a luscious sign

# INDUSTRIAL COLLAR, ANOTHER DOLLAR

I just needed a moment to slightly disappear
Unseen to seen, can't believe I'm right here
Conquering obstacles as the void tugs
It's only logical to leave it to powers above

I know this effort, tears and sweat
Paves the way for potent checks
What am I willing to sacrifice more?
Uneasy feeling, the end is 40 years more

Bills, thrills and fields of rain-kissed daffodils
Fuck a mill, give me prioritization with no guilt
The head is a lonely place unless you in bed
I read the victory we aim to taste is layers shed

Generational trauma left in the wake
Absence of my momma, but I concentrate
Poem after poem, hot shower, hour after hour
Scars shown, industrial collar, another dollar

# UNHOLY

You should know me
I reckoned better
All that is owed to me
Borrowed sweaters

Maleficent grin
Perceive, but directed
Can't really swim
Idolizations intercepted

Steady we went
Tides are much higher
Rose from the cement
Maybe I'm the liar

I'll bite that bullet sent
For my sake not yours
Entangled once again
Guess envy provokes lore

# Dear Mr. Blurryface

I poured one out for the homies as I usually do
Shadow looted, tripping over the laces of shoe
Beacon of light and a higher power's might
Breath of life in sight yet woes usually spite

Stifling shades, I'm a royal purple hue
Ego enraged, I'm nothing like you
Mind disturbed in hours late
My condolences to you Mr. Blurryface

This place not my home nor state of mind
Reaping of what was sown, passion divine
Rhetorical question, do you mourn friends too?
I poured one out for the homies as I usually do

# Nobody As One Would Say

I see capacity without the need to run in circles
Rationale being is my soul is the colour purple
Not the one to let the sarcasm faze easily
With these sorrowful days it's hard to breathe

Roll me one, I need salvation of some sort
Pour me one, retaliation with no need to resort
I fall in love with you especially in October
Pressure is the boulder, divinity not sober

Where we come from, it's all cut and dry
Summer sun, but luck is the art of getting by
I continue to love you in every which way
Cursed with pain, I'm nobody as one would say

Shawayne D                    June 23 2024

# SUBURBIA UNDISTURBED

"What has abundance brought you?"
P's and Q's, soiled shoes and exhaustion
"Choices you refused as they're talking"
I'm not mocking, but I believe in more

"White picket fence and doormat at the door"
Forget about rent, give me everything here
"The fear is that greediness might interfere"
I deserve it, flooded wrist and porch to sit

"That's a wish, but soul in exchange for it?"
Maybe all I desire is simply unheard
"My brother, that is suburbia undisturbed"

# WHAT I WAS GOING TO SAY

I hurt too
Capsizing into distortion
Words few
But we see healing is important

I ran the race
Bloody shoes
Guilt stricken face
What did I do to you?

Does it matter
After we've dined and laughed
Connection into disaster
Can you please take off the mask?

It's you beneath
Wanting to see me bleed till I drop
Didn't even speak
When arrogance consumed and shells—
*pop*

# SKIN TO SKIN

Your body rising
With each breath
Craving you beyond sex
Perhaps a lifetime or so

Can't convince my shadow
To follow me into the dark
But for you I'd lay down my heart
With tolerance of longevity and abundance

This whole affection thing doesn't make sense
Yet we still give it a go in the summertime
I watch possibilities evolve in your eyes
Laughter breaks layers of my dystopian soul

Never imagined making it work with no gold

# SOLSTICE INTERLUDE

Pattern of teardrops
Rumination suddenly
When does pain stop?
I am my greatest enemy

You could never imagine—
There I go assuming again
Not together as fathomed
In reality, we are not friends

This is bitterness sowed
Like a moth to the light
Pessimism unfolds in rows
Touch Earth without sight

May tomorrow bring
Unity understood anew
Not blood, but we can sing
I see your healing, Ayoku

# BTW

You aren't
The only one
We didn't start
Dismiss the weapon

I feel present
With a joyful crowd
Being is sufficient
Soul silent, ego loud

May the pain
Finally halt all of its deceit
When it rains
You walk on grass with feet

Wholeheartedly I tumble
Into many overdue hugs
As a unit we fully crumble
Sanctified of the bitter bug

# CUBICLE

Show me love
With no commission
Faith in what's above
Forward is the decision

Bills don't pay themselves
Or at least not in this chapter
How can we build wealth
When our goals met with laughter?

Ladder with plenty of snakes
Jargon be the demeanour
And with the unjustified hate
Blood on collars isn't cleaner

I see what I know
Disregarding grass on the other side
Stuck in this cubicle
Making the choice considered unwise

Shanapel                    June 23 2024

# YUDI

Brazen disregard of stress
How far will this check stretch
I guess less...but plenty some
I chose to reflect, you chose to run

Hopefully August flowers wither not
Defeat of the lust before death *pop*
Suddenly in the dark place with no light
Exhaustion the shadow, love the might

Chapter turned on what could've been
Lessons learned or we would've dimmed
Virtue pure nevermore with worldly woes
I stand by you in the space between rainbows

# PERCY

Valley of destitution
I rebuke the confusion
If sought is my downfall
I scoff cause we still ball

Elevate the mind state
You can't win and lack faith
Stomach once rumbled viciously
I may have tumbled, but rose to my feet

This jungle is unfavourable
For me to stay would be a miracle
I will in fact see you down the road
Nerves relaxed, but toad in my throat

# PURE

Disbelief how my will is weak
Purgatory without eternal sleep
Slayed the beast of discomfort
Pure creativity, but money comes first

Quarter to the time of rapture
Forgot to eat amongst disaster
I can't speak on the sensitivities
Pure volume in the silence we speak

Body tensed in concrete jungle
They introduced me to a life humble
If there pain, wrap meaningfully slow
Pure irony in solitude, crooked teeth show

# QUARTERS AND ONES

Slumber wherein eyes dart around
Not sure if I'm floating or on the ground

Switch the dough, eyes low in the matrix
Laughed off quick yet I pray I'm equipped

Did I just assume all the things like ball runs?
How I blinked with the thought I'd see the sun

More or less on the decompress with rum
Mercy me slow cause I'm the forgotten plum

# BAD ENERGY

Heal my body
Heal my mind
Whether you be prodigy
Or moral unrefined

Giving up my woes
Abundant, but dire
I try to stay ten toes
Upon concrete with tires

Taught to steer
Cause there be potholes
Succumbing to fear
Proves this life is a joke

Your smile morphs to frown
This time into the next
If I wanted to settle on down
I would have married my ex

# I Volunteer You

Make this world a better place
Rather than sit back and complain
Dance as it rains despite questions of sanity
Hold our hands and speak on unity unseen

When it gets dark I want to see you beam
Generosity and comfort for generational hurt
Some way, some how, you'd make it work
Cleanse the souls of those tainted with curse

I have the nerve to wish you a brighter future
Appreciate your worth, vocalize truest words

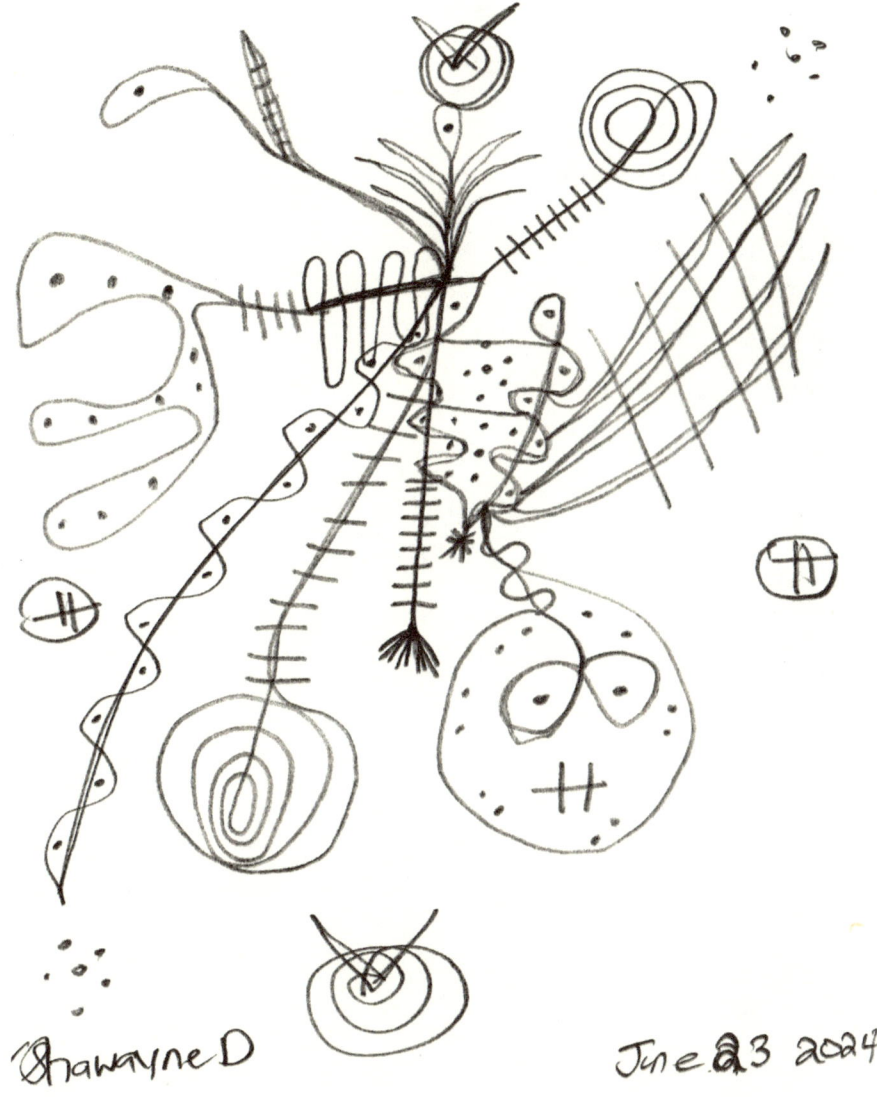

ShawayneD                    June 23 2024

# 12:54 IN PETERBOROUGH

You remind me
Of fire opal in October
Burning in my hands
I could never understand

What you saw in me
Good amongst a cruel society
But you were broken and torn
We were two sides of the coin

I am healing still in my own way
I am far, but you are further away

# EQUILIBRIUM

Hope resurrected
I stand corrected
On previous shortfalls
More or less hitting a wall

I've been with closure unresolved
I know of abandonment unsolved
I reckon what we do right is to heal
Believe when I say all of that was real

Real blockage in the flow of balance
In the mirror shouldn't provoke challenge
Questions heard, but interference takes time
I can't find the words to express how I'm—

# M.G.M

Tell them how is
Momma rose no fool
And when life constantly shifts
You somehow manage to keep cool

Profile vibes shed from our eyes
Our faith resides in ways you compromise
Time, effort and persistent spirit
If you've been haunted, we want to hear it

Been the dawg throughout pitfalls
I see your potential in the summer hue
And if there is no fear at all
We believe you will motivate those around you

Keep it going even when smiles turn to sobs
You know who you are, a member of the squad
Let me reinforce the trust and eternal hope
Coming together is how the community copes

# OVER MY HEAD

Weight of what was sought, but never found
I find myself sinking slowly into the ground

In over my head, I probably should stay in bed
Trying to get ahead, but I'm pulled at the thread

So it seems, self love the weapon that gleams
I'm amazed at powers above, faith in divinity

If you're listening please know I'm scared too
The vision defies bitterness that runs through

# 12:23 IN NIAGARA

This is more or less the unusual
But I rather be here in the flesh with you
Taking in the sights in this hotel room
Chocolate covered strawberries and tunes

Really though, I fall in love with you slow
Can't hold you to myself thus I let you glow
Quirks are a perk to blissful chemistry
We try to make it work while they disagree

Focused on cementing a legacy in my prime
They keep on walking when you draw the line
Daily routine, problems and opponents' unseen
As we asked for clarity they mistook prosperity

Shower me with your blessings and knowledge
Remind me of Sunday mornings and porridge
Fulfillment in knowing you're part of life's page
I cleanse my environment with a bit of sage

# AVOIDANCE PT. 2

I sense the distance with no resistance
You were coy and made in God's image
I prayed for joy and understanding with touch
I guess the bitterness took hold of both of us

Subway train, I like it when it rains
Eternal pain traded for passive shame
I wonder if your voice resonates laughter
My muttering turned into silence then after

Beautiful day, I prefer beautiful dawn
Leveling up is the vibe we're on
Not even sure why you came to mind
I reckon in this moment I too draw the—

Shawayne D                    June 23 2024

# THE BLINDS ARE BREATHING

My inhibitions cloaked as white serpents
Undeserving of experiencing this working
Need for closure intensifies amid routine
If I bring all the pain, showcase maturity clean

Unprovoked by the slightest mishaps
Energy in this room is all that I have
To be here true and in no moment other
Nonchalantly few seconds I would alter

Abundance sought for decades
Sentimental nod for the human race
Steady be the pace to peace of mind
There's love all around and we still got time

The blinds are breathing in unison with you
Lemongrass and eucalyptus cutting through
Possibility of anything less than a good day
Art as my outlet yet you'll heal in your own way

# IF NOT ME THEN WHO

Dropping these books like heads in church
Maybe you'll look at the result of overdue birth
I make it work with the opposition in the mirror
Figment of my imagination, the future is clearer

Holding it down while ever so far from you
Comfort without sound, I'm hurting too
I should be writing better, ain't my first rodeo
Heard its sweater weather, I'm better off alone

Microphones yearning story of a black protege
Dial tone left in the wake of forbidden soliloquy
Tiredness harnessed as the human condition
Failures tarnish thought I'd make a difference

They want purity, maturity and facts all centre
No need for apologies, I will be remembered
Tender be hands that draw close amid turmoil
Please understand the rise is mirrored by fall

# SOUBHIYÉ

Still in love with cotton candy skies
I reckon a younger me is proud indeed
I have the honour of calling you my why
Restoration of hope in all of humanity

This place is silent and joyous yet temporary
I feel the energy, I know desertion and hurt
Safety in the form of eyes pleading love free
Born in the concrete jungle, I rose from dirt

Hope for a change with no crying nor pain
I wish to pay the day back tenfold one day
Race and cycle are bound to leave us drained
I'm happy for now and for now that's okay

Bed is comfortable yet I hold capacity to rise
And welcome everything and nothing possible
I wash my face, brush teeth and close eyes
A silent prayer to overcome all obstacles

I would like family and friends to be good
I would like strangers to see me when I greet
Another notch, another chance, another hood
I wish you good morning even if we don't meet

# MAP

Whisper of a mountain
Subtle gentle breeze
Ice patches around
I take time to breathe

What lies on horizon
Pain inherited by nature
I am a virtuous son
Failure is not my full worth

Capable to analyze
I see more for now
Depression used to reside
Turn frown upside down

A voice cuts through
Closure is residual
Beauty when we meet in the middle
I see the capacity in you

Remind yourself you are worthy
See youth, glimmer and poetry

# Rosebud Hug

Staircase of a mind
Levels in this life
Peace may you find
Might not have twice

I plead a better story
Death is a tragic figure
Lack of optimism bores me
A good heart makes me a winner

The prize is rather dire
I tried to speak of it then
Guilty by association prior
You need clarification on the end

Restoration when you'd smile
I've been alone in the dark
I carry tragedy mile for mile
Vices extinguish the spark

Indifferent for love
Needing lessons dear
Formidable rosebud hug
I do not wish you were here

# PEACE AND ALIGNMENT

Why worry of what isn't present
To get here took many lessons
Hard times in fact, I'd rather not backtrack
To moments of fear in which I thought I lacked

Worthiness to be here, I see your pain
If no one said it, I care and see you're drained
It ain't no game when I ask you to breathe
Bad at mediation, but this puts mind at ease

Gratitude stretches to a younger you
For choosing to push on through
The lows which transformed to highs slowly
And if that time didn't come, I'm so sorry

As human in mortal coil I see you as one
My eye was closed, but now it's open
I would tell you of the self healing and hope
Now is a time of listening about how you cope

Stralayne D                                    June 25 2024

# Shadow Of the Shadow

Thankful for the wisdom yet curiosity remains
Look how far I've come, but who is Shawayne?
The poet, the lover, the friend willing to listen
The open, the unuttered, the cook in kitchen

I'm learning different methods of coping
What is written doesn't reflect what's spoken
I give onto you, virtue and mindful hesitancy
Sorry that you were hurt too, please be free

Lemongrass on the mantle, sandalwood candle
Relaxed attitude, I can not stay mad at two
Loving myself is where it starts, light in dark
Trauma dealt to the heart, daggers on mark

I feel for you, but I say please be free
One thing true, I protect my energy
I try to be a gentle fellow, gracious at hello
Sadly some can not go, shadow of the shadow

# ALMOND BUTTER

But I see now more than before
Trudging through mud to reach core
I'm distraught at reality that be
Can you hear one out and listen to me

Skin like desert and hunger on par
Truffle does its work along with Pinot Noir
I'm bound to go far after grimy state
I was given scars when I showed up late

Vocation apparent on the edge of destitution
I pray for my parents, may hope soothe them
What are we doing in this world that swirls?
Am I truly father figure to baby boy or girl?

In cold winters I tell stories with no stutter
Made things work in search of almond butter

# AFK

So entangled with all I wrote
I can't relax or grab remote
Clouded with smoke be the mind
Exposure of self, the lesser kind

Whiplash at quarter to 1
Couldn't dash so block spun
No cause only actions today
Battle at a loss when AFK

I resurrect emotions faint
Come correct if you be saint
I believe in people and love being lethal
Darkness is residual, reason I'm single

I can not blame society nor you
Heart will be at ease as I see this through
Let there be understanding in shadows of bliss
Batteries you didn't bring so the shots miss

# LIKE WATER

I breathe the air you breathe
May rejuvenation empower we
I see change on the mantle
On a fortnight, I lit a candle

I remember nights not long ago
Quiet home, hot coco and somber snow
Bestowed were hopes of prosperous holidays
But right now there is chaos in the wake

Of industrial necessity
Climate change compromising peace
Fingers pointed like weary markers
In the midst of pain, I say love, like water

Flow between cracks
Empower with compassion and laughs
We might not have all and then some
But the virtue we carry should not leave world with
breadcrumbs

On hazy days, snowmen fall
When I was a kid they stood tall
As an adult I analyze with my coffee
Looking at streets and trees, snowless and empty

I heard it goes in a cycle
Repercussions are trivial
Maybe one day it'll work out

Maybe I'm a mere poet, so there's still doubt

Hands balled while the world purple
Saving grace for lonesome turtles
Nothing changes if we don't care
The result is no elephants or polar bears

Like water, rise and gush
Like water you are enough
Like water, you'll find a way
Like water, you'll replenish and hydrate

# FOREIGN

Land of possibility, a place in the sky
I was born to be free and that's far from a lie
I can't imagine making it there rather within
Would the creator disagree that I'm free from sin

Hopes and dreams along sleeve of destitution
I took time to grieve words they were using
World gone belly side up and there's no hope
But I believe change begins with us and that's no joke

Conscious efforts
Plain and simple
Conscious efforts
Understanding is residual

Conflict amuck
I pluck the tip of stagnation from flesh
Tired of feeling stuck
And agreeing this is as good as it gets

We are people
Having a lived experience
If ignorance is lethal
Can you blame us for caring?

For not slinking away despite rain pouring
Made it to foreign, now healing is important
Digress from stress that it all gets worst
The beauty in the struggle is self reflection first

VAnawayne D                    June 25 2024

Food insecure
Environments poor
Pollution on the floor
Oh I can list a couple more

Collapsing icebergs
Displaced hurt
Rising debt that unfurls
And yet despite it all I find beauty in this world

We can make a difference
For generations inbound
My neighbours and friends
There's love all around

If we come direct
And put mine to passion
We defeat the threat
Of self destruction beyond imagination

# DESERT BLUE, I FALL FOR YOU

Wherein we rise, we fall eventually
September eyes on all hollow's eve
I need to be free from stress haunting me
Summer breeze and sex on the beach

Could be the view or Caribbean Sea
Desert blue, mirages I tend to see
I fall for you wholeheartedly amid shame
Grip of fear never loose, I feel your pain

Parameters broken; lessons learnt
The saga of ocean, bridges burnt
Might as well quit while I'm ahead
Could this be bliss, stolen kiss in bed?

Ain't worthy, wonderment while gazing at trees
Desperation at the seams, on shoulder I lean
You are perfection, so why doubt your love?
Moment of detection, hands full of blood

# COMPLAIN

Why pockets be empty
Why they drain my energy
Why do we tend to disagree
Why not a couple m's around me

Why is the sky blue
Why do I resent you
Why couldn't I see it through
Why tell seed be born anew

Why hunger never cease
Why do I philanthropy weak
Why did I suffer defeat
Why mind never at ease

Why this and that
Why future I never had
Why do I feel pain of my dad
Why y'all telling me don't be sad

Why the world in conflict
Why I need to top my old shit
Why search in lieu of profit
Why worry about world when God got it

# WOLFPACK

Life lessons that led here today
Countless blessings after I saw grey
Survival together or balance lone self
Dismal type weather, born with no one else

I never could have imagined connections
Those willing to dive in with no hesitation
Lonely while not alone is a repercussion
Being not fine isn't brought up in discussion

I want you to win as true as the moon's glow
To my next of kin, we are roots for seed below
The hunger, snow and devastation alleviated
I speak gratitude for the next generation

For which I lack I'm thankful for pack
Acceptance we sat in present and looked back
May no tribulation compromise relations
I'm elevated, but I will join against dictation

# LAZY BONE

No sympathy, no disillusion nor denial
Self destruction, bitter means and closed eyes
I fortify assumptions with lack of self doubt
Courage of mentioning unfazed by mouths

Round and round be the dance of life
I hit the ground before you told me do it twice
Lustful intentions of making it to the other side
Hard for me to entertain souls unlike mine

My brother, my sister, my unenlightened friend
No other mister who finds you in the end
Capable of breaking stagnation and chains
I'm no saviour, but mere poet who is Shawayne

Prideful snow, melodic echo, got lazy bone
Close the show, distorted flow, where is home?
Candle flame, repeated name, will still weak
Constant shame, love untamed, we are free

# VANILLA ORANGE

Flesh I couldn't forget so I come direct
Fistful of dreams and generational stress
Reminiscent of rain outside and liquor pouring
See you in the morning, gift of vanilla orange

I feel you when you're not here in this room
All we've been through; I hope you come soon
The tune of Machiavelli, I find myself scary
Bones are weary, rattling before you see me

I grieve a younger me on lonesome days
When I rise, Palo Santo essence on face
A time ago I was told to wash feet and pray
Looked death in the eyes and said not today

Ancestors proud and family too, baby cheerful
Should I go back to school when life's good?
Questions with no answer now, come again
Chocolate storm, tender hue, here we begin

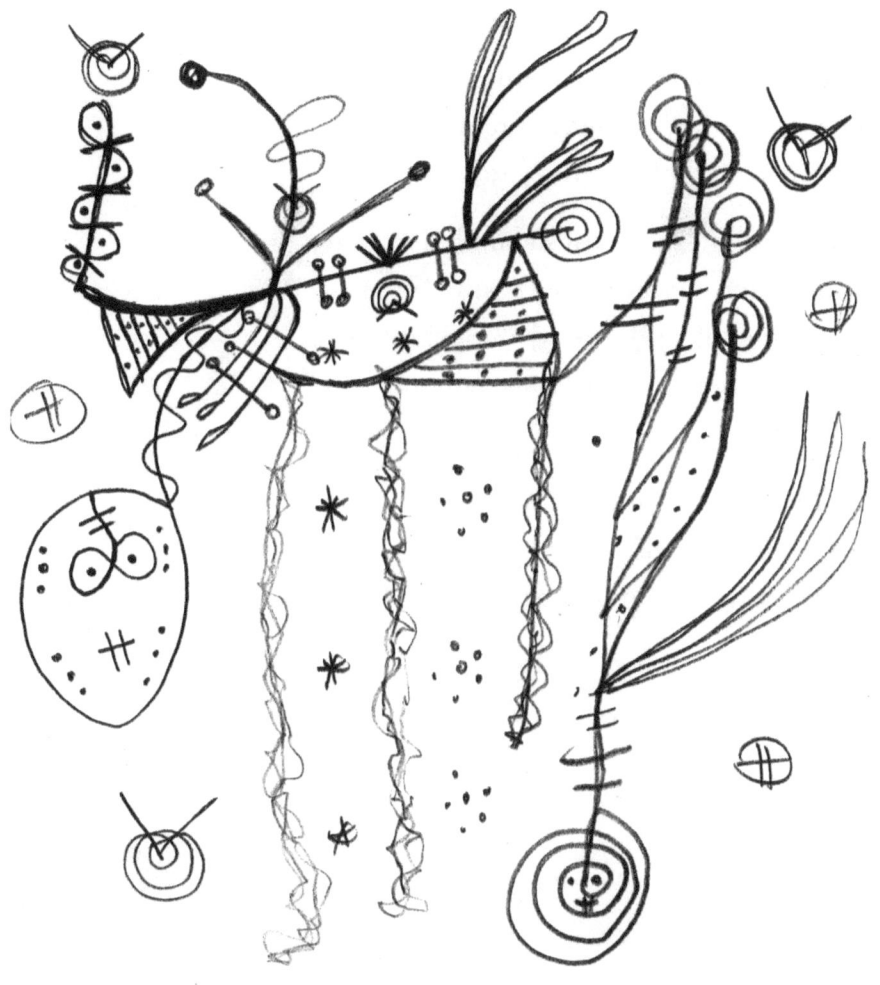

Shawyna D                                    June 25 2024

# OSMOSIS

Trust that knowledge will arrive in time
Ancestral guidance and virtue
If there is darkness please do shine
I'm sorry for whatever hurt you

Divinity pulling us from cemented notions
I fell back for a second here and there
Loving yourself is the most important
Wherein that process I know you care

To value me as one and enough
So as this poem begun, it will end with trust
Chaotic mindset yet you're passing through
Osmosis is the emotion, bare yourself anew

# FUPPERNICKEL

I see what we can be wholeheartedly
I know I can achieve if I just focus on me
The necessity of means to stay afloat
Righteous I'm deemed as they nod as I spoke

There is hope even if it be a sliver
I should hold you when you shiver
I could be further with an aptitude of dreams
I choose to be a merger of love and streams

No apology today for you need to heal
I should fall for the sway of comfort to feel
Everything in every which way beyond realm
I know in this moment I'm mellow and blem

I pray for you beneath misty skies
To say the times aren't missed is a lie
We were young, we were naive, we were little
World spun, I left with the breeze, Fuppernickel

# MANGO SEED

Guilty by association
Before being dashed into ocean
I open wounds in front of you
You plead pacifism on a Tuesday

Work hard just to play amongst mountains
That stood before 1999, I resent change
Penny for thoughts as I try to swim
In the destruction of my own doing

Where do my people go when curtains close?
Reaped what I sowed just to capitalize
I'm no better than some less fortunate
I reckon we're all going through it

You give me time when sun don't shine
I'm provoked to slink off into dark
Be the flame without dim nor flicker
Mango seed behind home of freedom

# REST ASSURED

There's love smiling on the horizon
There's inside jokes waiting to be shared
There's outfits to be discovered
There's laugher worth waking up neighbours

There's food and drink combinations
There's moments to cry and stutter
There's hikes eager to be conquered
There's hope in the ambiguity of tomorrow

There's pain right now
There's faith within
There's hunger for knowledge
There's mortal coil for blessings

There's a time and a place
There's shame we don't speak of
There's disconnection and human obsession

There's all these reasons...so hold on please

# SPALINQCY MILLER

Heart black as skin
Sins chased with gin
Lust and trust in tow
Compassion breaks rope

Uncomfortable denial
She is one with child
Society seen at fault
American Dream bolts

Awoken at table
A prayer if I'm able
Throat course right now
She clawed from upside down

Rose in concrete
I speak a poem sweet
For friend turned stranger
If sharing is caring, you bring danger...

# CINNAMON TOAST

Gratitude for the day as I wake
Change is the ripple effect I create
Blossoming hues, the sky is my muse
I fade into blue, appreciation no use

Somber tone in home that mocks vulnerability
I pick up the phone as clock stares at me
Remedies for dystopian children alike
War of worlds, may we love with no spite

No opposition in mirror yet something missing
The well wishes became clear when I listened
The last of '99, we are kindred folk
May future be sublime as cinnamon toast

rawayneD                                    June 25 2024

# THE HUMAN CONDITION

Falling behind, but right on time
I am the colour blue and red combined
Nothing for certain, but that's a deadly finger curl
Beyond the hurting, I find hope in this world

# SHADOW

"You look like flavorful mornings of opportunity true. I'm always on the move, but I'll always make time for you."

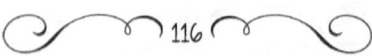

# WUNDERKIND

One day you gon' make your momma proud
Standing on stages with cheers from the crowd
One day you gon' make all the haters see
That negativity will lead to eternal defeat

One day you going to amplify all of us divine
A brother in blood encapsulated in wunderkind
One day you will fall in love with yourself
Each day is great cause health is wealth

# HALF BAKED SO YOU FLAKE

Not how it seems, but what I deem and ponder
You've been wasting my time since November
Tried to it make work, but same old, same old
The thing that hurts is all the apologies I told

Pity me not, into this letter I jot
May everything you desire rot as you plot
Scarred to a degree, never could be me
In reality, you were born for the streets

Dodging storms and daggers you throwing
Weaponized words with no context nor form
The world is yours to create, master the faith
Told you save the date, half baked so you flake

# RELATIVE IN THE SPIRIT

Spiritual guide, miracle maker
Ancestors from the land of Jamaica
Like the great ones, passion takes labour
I'm the plum, dark skin ain't doing favours

Spiritual guide, miracle maker
Let me speak to all of the haters
Ego tame, but the voice spews pain
How far I came while they were swerving lane

Dog in a cage, I need to be free
Dues are paid yet there lies envy
What you're telling me is to a lesser degree
Ain't nothing capable of stopping creativity

It is what it is like the time on the clock
Vulnerability isn't accessible to the block
What must be known is how we love you lots
Spiritual guide, miracle maker, I too am lost

# It Don't Rhyme Pt. 4

Lemongrass and Sage
Beautiful aroma innit
I'm jealous of the rain
Joy without you is possible

Lotus in a tender hue
Bestow your burdens to me
Obligations and confusion dire
We live in a—constant race

Allow divinity to intervene
Lonely beyond comprehension
Smokey clouds with no direction
I find peace in your healing

Why can't my heart accept compassion?
I bleed chaotic nostalgia and inner turmoil
Perhaps they're disgusted at the rose
I shun the envy that stems from resentment

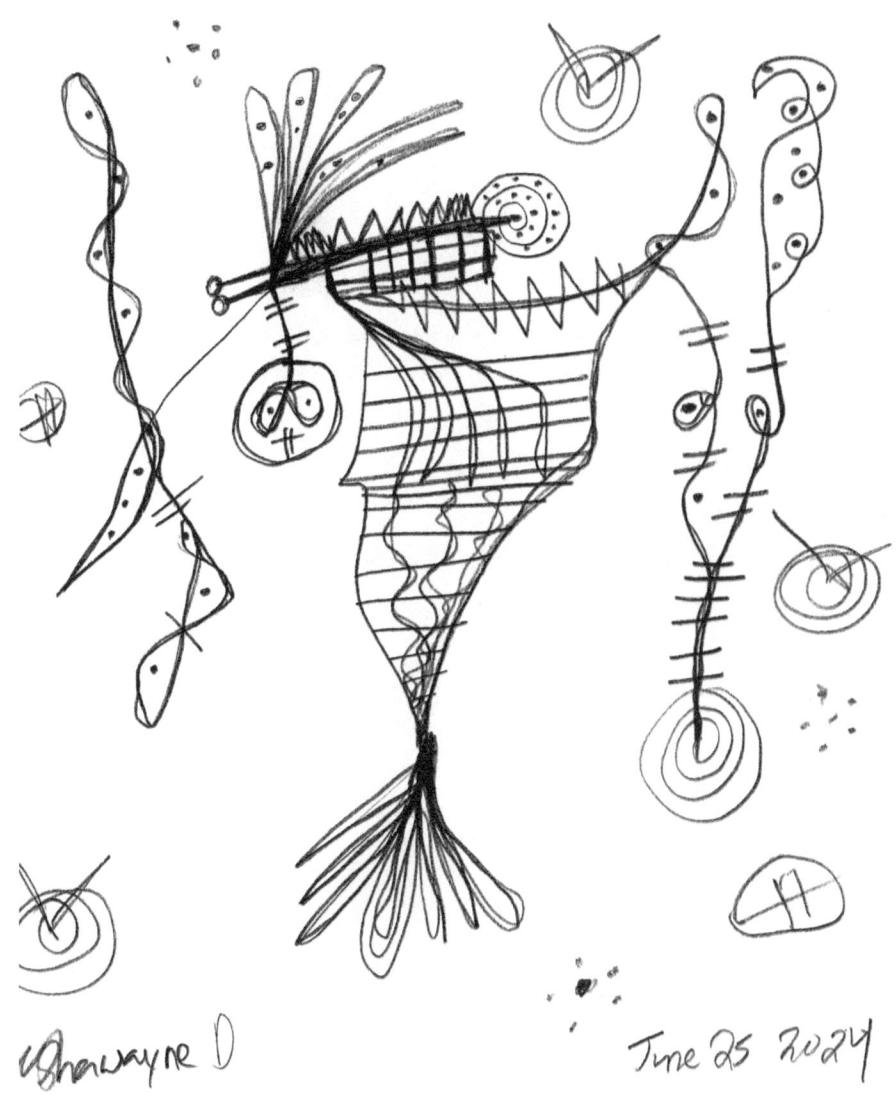

Shawayne D                                    June 25 2024

# MORNING AFTER

Room's a mess
Head on chest
Partner in crime
I think so, I guess

Pushing 24
Show me love
Beyond photos
Abandonment tugs

Grip weakens
Rise through cement
Resort to compassion
We are all merely human

Connection on a deeper
They may not love you either
Nothing less than a shared moment
"Hello...goodbye. It was nice to meet you"

# LYCHEE AND LANDMINES

Mellow minded voice
Turned course when it worsens
My insults are spelled in cursive
If you're the boy then I'm the serpent

Cornrows with more history
Than a wannabe with pure mystery
I spew wickedly to your dome piece
Ghetto terminology about to send you deep

Beneath the concrete or into to the sky
Be my guest as you decide the fate of life
Eat the lychee, but beware the landmines
Next to the tree are signs of those less kind

# BIZARRE

Before you could ask I was long gone
I didn't fear your wrath, I feared holding on
What's the point in hoping with much emotion?
I met you when I was broken

I was left with my heart ripped open
Cigars toking will gradually reveal
That my mind has noted you're simply not real
Just a figment of my complexed imagination

Tsk tsk I digress, this is merely a conversation
With the inner voices and shadows vexed
Bizarre choices for what I'm about to do next
"You're so happily the living proof..."

Then why am I constantly in the same loop

# I Come in Peace

You're not eager to see me
But that's okay, I don't like me as well
My dawgs deserve prosperity
The hearse haunting though life going swell

Battled demons, migraines and disillusion
Generosity in the words I'm using
Pour me one slowly and straight up in fact
If this is all delusion then lessons I will stack

I come in peace no matter colour nor creed
I come in peace no matter lover nor seed
I come in peace even if the time arrives to cry
I come in peace even if the signs tell you to fly

# LAVISH

But I deserve it though
Island sun with hair in cornrows
Peace of mind and dough
Type of lifestyle you see in photos

People wearing the merch
Since birth I knew about hurt
Tried to make it work, closure needed
Flower from the dirt, healing is the secret

Possibility to make you happy
Since birth you knew of grief
Million-dollar dreams, pockets of dimes
Not as pure as you see, don't fall for lines

Moment to represent for the fallen
Speak sense to me before ashes ascend
Hard work before opportunity came calling
This is motivation for all of my amazing friends

# Amor

You know who you are
Type of energy of a star
Wiser than a lot of entities
You ignite the passion in me

Give me a tour of your mind
Shoulder to lean on when not fine
Hope defined as uplifting your heart divine
Let me run you a bath and pour some wine

Cashmere or not, come here to the spot
Elegance and relevance making me jot
Elaborate vocation during sunsets
Thankful for patience, my best kept secret

SharynD                                    June 26 2024

# WHEN I'M BACK

I see now what was left behind
Tears in your eyes are the sign
Hope refined as the force that binds
Tender lies when I elaborate I'm fine
Slight discourse, what's worse than that?

# TALISA

You been the one since the get go
Allow me to shelve the lonesome ego
Winds that blow with burdens in tow
How far we go, that's good to know

I've been meaning to elaborate
This evening I wanted to conversate
On all your greatness in pure motion
You're the moon, I'm the rhythmic ocean

Pen to paper I jot after a while
Time the teacher, I'm the ignorant child
Maybe you wonder why I took time to write
A letter of intent for you walking out my life

# ELEPHANT

In the room
In the tomb
I confuse the fumes
Winter coming soon

Might as well
Put forth myself
Stuck in a daze prior
You ignite soulful prayers

Don't need a lecture
Fed up with pressure
Gratitude back to source
I shouldn't be your last resort

# THAT'S OKAY... IT'S JUST A BAD DAY

How could I not spin the block?
Homie shot so heart just rot
No time for interrogation about hurting
Trust me, this second I'm not the bigger person

How could I not soak in all the fear?
She chose to leave as I started to care
I feel what I feel with no jury nor judge
25 to life, I'm not accustomed to hugs

How could I not be driven to sob?
Hands trembling in response to the job
I'm more asleep than awake for the future
Steps that I take, but I'm not Martin Luther

How could I not let you down again?
Claims of how you're a worthy friend
Tribulations in every which way around
Discomfort true with no reason nor sound

# IMPLOSION

Needed merely a sec to come direct
Smoking on your cigarette
Middle finger to lonely death
I'm Casper with no silhouette

I'm the biggest threat
Fuck your picturesque
I backtrack then 2 step
Nearly collapsed before Jah intercept

"Shaweezy, patience is the secret"
No sweat despite fear that crept
Masked face bent on distress
Here's your flowers for boasting like the rest

The implosion of reckless coasting and stress

# SEE YOU YESTERDAY

"Take the hint"
It hurts to think
"I'm here for you"
I wish that were true

"Blame the world not affection"
Where were you when I lacked direction?
"It's a pity the holes we dig deep"
Bury me with tears and reciprocity

"I wish for you to be present, but great"
I'm undertaking lessons so see you yesterday

Shawyne D                                    June 26 2024

# THE INFLUENCE OF INDIFFERENCE

Made to illuminate timid souls
I trade my pain for gold and candid photos
Fuck a no show, I need divinity to intervene
My generation loco, but I'm a hypocrite indeed

What's an island to a nation? Gentrification...
Childhood sounds foolish to bloody money
When we slip up it ain't nothing funny
Can't even sit back and pleasurably relax

Drones in the air, but certain is death and tax

# BABY BURGUNDY

I meant what I said
And I said what I meant
Don't pry into my head
Certainly not paying rent

It was a displeasure to meet
See me better, don't speak
Taking care led me here
I chose to utterly persevere

I left you down in a pass life
I reckon the frown cause I'm nice
Forward is the motion, midnight toasting
Healing body broken with peace unspoken

# PRIDE

I'm not who you say
But I'll sit back and wish you a better day
Trigger fingers itching to see us bleed
Wise man once said, "We live in a society"

All my dreams manifest as I take on lessons
Shooting your shot, but you're not Beckham
Ain't a threat so I come direct to protect
Less talk, more stress, don't know poverty yet

I'm on the charts, they didn't start
I'm on TV, they studying my history
Blocking left and right, microscope on my life
I'm the approachable guy, quote to live by

We taking trips like we ain't young and shit
Never mind the whip, I'll get there by ship
Jokes aside, pride exist in eyes of mine
Laws abide, but glory reside in the dime

# 8PM IN SAUGA

I forgot how much I missed you
Till just then
I've got acquaintances more than a few
But you are my best friend

I said I loved you
In a moment of ego letdown
May the October hue
Remind you of love all around

Missions and adventures
I'm quite a spontaneous guy
The world revolves not, for you are the centre
Please spread your wings and fly

May this poem wrap and flow
Like the waves of the Pacific Ocean
Lake Ontario is what we know
But I imagine you get the notion

# MOUNTAIN IN THE CLOUDS

My rock, my foundation
Here in this spot, teach me elevation
Beyond time and money, can't forget effort
The distance is funny, yet I reckon it can work

Wicked potions have been the notion
The herbs are the ancestral remedy
Being with you lures me into the open
Alas, you shall exist after my memory

Wolfsbane and sage casted down
I am in a position no better
Seeping out their pockets as they ring round
Birds do flock together

I can't guarantee making you proud
I'm working on the ego slow
You are a mountain in the clouds
Being with you is seemingly—

# LEFT, LEFT, RIGHT

I choose gratitude over attitude
I'm no longer that guy
I can't even stay mad you
Or ensure you touch the sky

Round of applause for the plot
Y'all been at it for some time now
The cause is for me to eternally rot
Closure is comfort without sound

4 bands, I know you tryna hustle
Warm hands, that never held nor loved you
Not sure why I bring the attention
To bitterness I usually don't mention

How much my life worth compared to you?
Spiritual guide, miracle maker, winter blues
The envy eventually strangles and spites
Out the door, timid core, left, left, right

Just Breathe

ShawneD                              June 26 2014

# YELLOW LIGHT

I hold my breath
Damsels in distress
Life force for the check
Imma need you to come correct

I hold my heart
Setup up from the start
Sleeping with the sharks
Love will lead you into the dark

I hold my head
Nimble be the thread
As I weave words never said
Sell not the soul to get ahead

I hold my tears
Capacity to die right here
Step into rather than run from the fear
In time the nerves settle, and pain disappears

I hold my tongue
Defeat imminent since I begun
Couple dollars for my daughters and sons
That ain't a bottle, rather a bullet from a gun

# POUR ME ANOTHER, LOST A BROTHER

Hellos into goodbyes too soon
We should be on a beach in Cancún
Butterfly in the cocoon, I gloom...
Filled up, yet I feel alone in this room

Blood unrelated to potent veins
I wish to celebrate walking you into fame
The crowd knows my name, lower the shame
You'd reckon I've changed, soaked up the pain

Blessings aplenty, see the good in me
Dodging envy, walking away should be easy
Trying to find my place in a flawed society
I am lost and she is quoting Ecclesiastes

# 5PM IN RICHMOND -INTERLUDE

I'm not arguing, this is a conversation
What change you bring? I reckon gentrification
Morning appreciation, porridge on the table
I see you need saving, unsure if I'm able

Too much the price to get right, crooked life
No change still in sight, I bleed apartheid
Red or blue pill, I don't choose sides
Is the soul worth a mill, price to get right

Born in the dirt, I weather your pain
Fondly searched, yet fell victim to blame
Cursed by bloodshot eyes, I'm no good
Not asked if alright, but risen up by the hood

I swallow shame, urging leniency for sins
When I go by Shawayne, the plot thickens
We've all got masks, beyond what they render
All that I ask, is for you to make it to December

# ARIANA'S LULLABY

For now there is sleep.
No monsters under the bed
No ill intentions to get ahead
No curses or dire circumstances
Only closed curtains and second chances

For now there is sleep.
No bills or lack of anything
No thrills or predicaments
No fires, wires, gas or smoke
Only pjs, milk, lullabies and hope

For now there is sleep.
No gossip about the things
No profit when fear clings
No astronomical gain wherein you shutter
Only a sleeping babe who knows you love her

# BOTANICAL

With roots
With truth
I pray for you
Living proof

Of purity
Innocence
Captivation
Deliverance

Greed retreats
Timid feet
Intolerant men
Beneath branches

Woven ships
Nectar filled sips
Silent wish
Poisonous kiss

# WALLS OF EDEN

How must I compare
To a lesser person
I'm still standing here
In the shadow of your hurting

I build you up
For them to tear down
My hands are scoffed
From kneading the ground

Foundation of roots
Pleasure lives elsewhere
Struggle is the truth
I'm no stranger to care

Vast and gleaming
A story unspoken
Walls of Eden
Home of the broken

Shawayne D                                    June 26 2024

# *AUTUMN*

Your colours remind me
That life isn't a bore
Brisk breeze when you
Enter the scene

My only wish is for
A couple more
Whispered to the trees
That life is a dream

# Wrong in the Neon

Something quite sinister
Pulls away the innocent rug
I traverse the foreign winter
Before Shaweezy was Tumblebug

Impromptu missions concerning
The mortal coil being temporary
Shadows continue burning
My soul hangs in purgatory

Be still my friend, be still my foe
Familiarity bares no power here
If this is the end, may you know
I lost my mind a moment there

Few days of mastered pinnacles
You can have almost all that's mine
Their world is less equal, but cynical
The vote is that I'm not quite fine

Life is a gem of synchronicities
Me wishing bad is not the right way
Underwhelming what was done to me
Karma is sitting by myself to pray

# FABRIC

Generational heirloom
Bestowed in bright rooms
Adjacent to gateways of trust
This is putting in labour unlike luck

I feel at peace to witness scene
Accolades sweet, I yearn desire
Inner fire content with community
Will be weak, is this purgatory?

I advocate the latter, trying my best
In absence of laughter, love I forget
My people, my neighbour, my friend
Hold me not lethal, be anchor in cement

Cape of desperado's lingering in wind
Swerving potholes wherein we sink
I'm no different than you in the pit of struggle
Rational being disassembles carefree bubble

# MAGENTA ON BLACK

Too many goodbyes amid soul search
If you be wise, keep in mind foes lurk
Tides passing by, I am rose to dirt
Shelter your pain, too close means hurt

Periodic despair, the rain amplifies
Fighting back tears, are you still my why?
Just wanted to settle and disappear like ghost
Now I'm climbing levels, anxiety still no joke

Drastic release of prior ego, I finally let go
Money come and go, living life is what we owe
Experiences amongst trials and tribulations
"Love...this world never asked for your saving"

I want them to be okay, no matter if I'm lost
I could give my entirety, but sanity be cost
And if you decide to hold and piece me back
You would understand magenta on black

# IKIGAI

The night it all happened it was truly hard
Sat at a window praying for clarity amid scars
You were far, ideology was I'd go home soon
Guilty as charged for losing my mind in room

I wished to settle down upon departure
Frown refused to turn around as hour lurked
The sound was my heart breaking close to 3
I was awaking to reality no one to save me

I missed you regardless of fate encountered
Casual smiles despite the animosity heard
I knew they were lost too, nothing to lose
I'm not your enemy, our hurting shares roots

Why is it that I believe in the good still?
The capacity of a lived life is to simply feel
I don't know, I'm just a side character in story
Pouring wholeheartedly so you see Ikigai

# Rock Salt

Mystification of the higher self
Change I'm creating leads to wealth
Bygones are bygones, gratitude true
Missed you before you were gone

October Blue
Exemplified in eyes is idea we can start anew
I must move ahead with only few
Jealousy still hate and love at same time

Stubborn understanding, you will never be mine
Meditation still no good, black boy meets 25
Can I tolerate growing up when I fear to die?
The question is if rather when, roots interfere

In the end are you my friend or will you disappear?
Milling through thoughts, I discover rock salt
Mind temporary locks off, mania the cost
I prayed for redemption beneath night sky

Snow underneath feet as I finally said goodbye

Shawayne D                    June 26 2024

# UNAVAILABLE

Poor me, poor my
Tears in my eyes
Eager to touch sky
Not eager to die

Repression of needs
I shall water seed
Be free along this journey
I might not be the one you need

Rediscovered spark
My image lingers in heart
Mirror to mature poser
If you feel pain, I've left mark

I will leave calm if I'm able
The emotions and future unavailable
No time of doubt in the budget debate
I find peace in the most lonesome state

# ECLIPSE OVER BRAMPTON

Train tracks lead back to a younger me
I unpack vulnerability, you pray to achieve
The fleeing of leaves within a new year
I promise with the wind I won't disappear

Otherwise known as greed, I atone with peace
Passed onto seed is legacy, be free into destiny
Idolization of welcomed fortune amid turmoil
I love with the power of the sun, water and oil

Minor confusion for what tomorrow may bring
Soul sings as the flickering flame doesn't dim
I awoke in a pool of lust and dire silence
Rupture between us initiated by violence

Communities aren't strangers to the mourning
I take a knee while adoring moonlight pouring
Illumination potent in chaotic balance of life
I'm here toasting that you get home alright

# HAND ME DOWNS

Some jays from the broski, summer never ends
Rumination to a younger me, we are friends
The tragic backdrop of struggle, choirs amuck
The gentrification will humble, we aren't stuck

Pockets affluent in dreams during journey far
If black boy doesn't scare, what's hoodie to car?
What's face to concrete? Why no speech?
If they rob the energy, may identity I keep

Heard the gossip and misadvise
I would be keen to swerve twice
Striding into future universe dictates suitable
I need to put in work, so you don't cry at funeral

Black boy fly amid the clouds with love found
It ain't no lie that I still carry hand me downs
If there's a chance, may bliss be compensation
Two for the dance, I hear divine conversation

# MID OCTOBER

I know I'll be happy
Some time down the line
Even if you disagree
I uphold that I'm fine

Balance in life and priorities
I'm energized by vibrant October moon
The demeanour may be meek
But the love I carry takes up this room

More everything to myself and my people
May it all be good with no repercussion
I once spoke about love that was lethal
Death was never in fact blushing

I'm sorry for the distance
My heart yearns journey back to self
The prayer of mine holds the most significance
Hopes of us being safe and full of wealth

# FAULT OF NONE

I can not blame the plot
Instead I release and jot
Melodic words about purpose
One with birds till I fade to stardust

Image refined through time
Two to sign before we intertwine
May love lead us along superior course
My heart does not blush at chance of divorce

Pennies and dimes in the past
Soon I'll be free from it all at last
Perhaps philanthropy and potlucks
When you have too much is it too much?

Lots of time for the task assigned
I encourage reader to enter my mind
Tour the bad wherein I defended good
Went from being sad to misunderstood

# Blurred Turquoise Lagoon

I never mentioned how I felt
Emotional ties back to a younger self
Midnight in my room, I tend to sloom
Morning hue welcomes you, abandon gloom

Like a wave of consciousness, I find peace
I know this isn't as good as it gets, heart leaps
The chance of it working out without doubt
For me to be role model with expression from mouth

Holes in a timid soul so I grip hope tenderly
Even if uncertainty provokes, let it free
Like the woes, like the birds, like the trees
If we come together perhaps there be unity

My vision is tunnel along unpaved path
If I'm not the first, I won't settle for last
I used to pray for you to come home soon
But all I see is blurred turquoise lagoon

Shawayne D                    June 26 2024

# 14:14

Well-being
Sought after
Like moth to flame
I am indifferent to pain

The routine
Of trauma for trauma
Addictive like marijuana
Focused on counting commas

My brother
In community and residual drought
My sister
Amongst foolery and inconceivable doubt

We are people
Having lived experience with room for healing
No need to be miserable
Your perseverance is a beacon revealing...

# CLEVER

When I think of you
Solutions arise for the obstacles
Gratitude becomes the attitude
Moving forward seems logical

I used to exist in pits of defeat
Submerged in the concrete
The focus was not on being ten toes
There was a ball of angst forming in throat

I need my people to win
Cleansed from sin and generational hurt
The capacity of diving in
Illuminates the struggle and mental worth

Hands of time, I lift problems to divine
May darkness know me no better
This light of mine intensifies
Love of one another is the choice clever

# BREADCRUMBS

There are highs
As there are lows
This world moves fast
So remember to breathe slow

# MATCHSTICK AND GENESIS

Stagnation is futile.
Might just have to turn back the dial
On passionate days and the beautiful sway
Of your essence in the summertime
I can't promise I won't let you down this time

I cried a river.
Wept till my face burned
Lessons I was to learn escaped in the moment
Sometimes I feel like a disappointment
Sometimes the image in the mirror turns out
To be not the opponent

Set me free.
The voice returned for those curious
I'm a pacifist so I shrug off the thought
Of being furious
The world can be potent, loving, but filled with Unjust
I'm just thankful to experience both of us.

# RESIDENCY

You aren't done.
May the glow of the sun empower you
Regardless of winter hues
That claim you should be forever miserable

I still believe in you
I spoke of struggle.
Wrapping my body in cocoon
Immortalized by Medusa

You're still the most important
Person in the room
May challenges not overtake you
Pride is the opposition.

May my children know worthiness tenfold
If we build the home of potential
I hope for the love not to be residual
My love is the unforgettable foreign delicacy

And I'm the starving artist advocating
Residency

# NESTIVIA

I don't write the same anymore...
Some would say that's a shame
But rather than proclaiming life a bore
I went out and gave the day a try

I'm a pretty notable guy
Pride and ego shaking hands
I hope to be the better man
If there's everything to lose

Weaponized fear
Strangles dreams on this holy morning
I can not claim sanctification
I'm merely human and I believe in the good

But even that could land me in a deep waters
I stride towards the alter of matrimony
If we start, may you accept me wholeheartedly
I agree to disagree on certain matters

Beautiful nations engulfed in laughter

Shawayne

June 26 2024

# IMPECCABLE

The heart has lied before
I believe the capacity is for us to soar
Above the negativity and such
I still love you so much

Words never spoken till recent
My shoulders have dirt, but the pockets decent
Can't be chasing rather attract then stack
Death came and I wasn't ready

So I pull life back
You've always been impeccable to me
You're elegant, but not eager about poetry
Ambitions of your own in a world cold

Maybe I should take a trip down memory road
The laughter, your smile and genuine tears
Even after the pain I will still be here
I don't write the same, yet you watch me jot

"Shaweezy, the game is to maintain your spot"

# BLINDS OF THE ABODE

Speaking truth in rooms, inner child proud
I'm used to all the gloom, I see your pain loud
Homecoming when I detach from self
No running when recognition brings wealth

I choose me without the grandiosity
Hands unclean with scars deep
The book nearly complete, cemented ten
If I weep at your feet, will you still call me friend

I heard the rumours been potent
Light to them illuminates lesser emotions
Amongst the ruins I was coping fair
Everything I was doing was to show I cared

Will the heart ever be settled after chaos
Look into my eyes and get lost
Told to be one with love, passion and hope
I feel like the forgotten son behind blinds of the abode

# LET THE DUST SETTLE

Voice course, I see the world needs healing
Change I can't force, but inner power revealing
I'm no spectator, intuitive values to draw back
Woes I bid later; fear is something I overlap

Shaweezy still within, the game needs no hero
If I were to broadcast sins, pulse runs to zero
Weaponized words before, dive into lore
Laziness I've heard more, move forward past closed door

May retaliation cease, we have worthy sleep
And if even I suffer defeat, I rose from concrete
Sing about me when I'm gone, yet not too quickly
It's a beautiful journey of life we're on, please stay with me

I idealize the thought of if I were to grow
Feeling lost, but I see the prize being rose
The emotions are like steam in a kettle
I plead devotion to gleam after dust settles

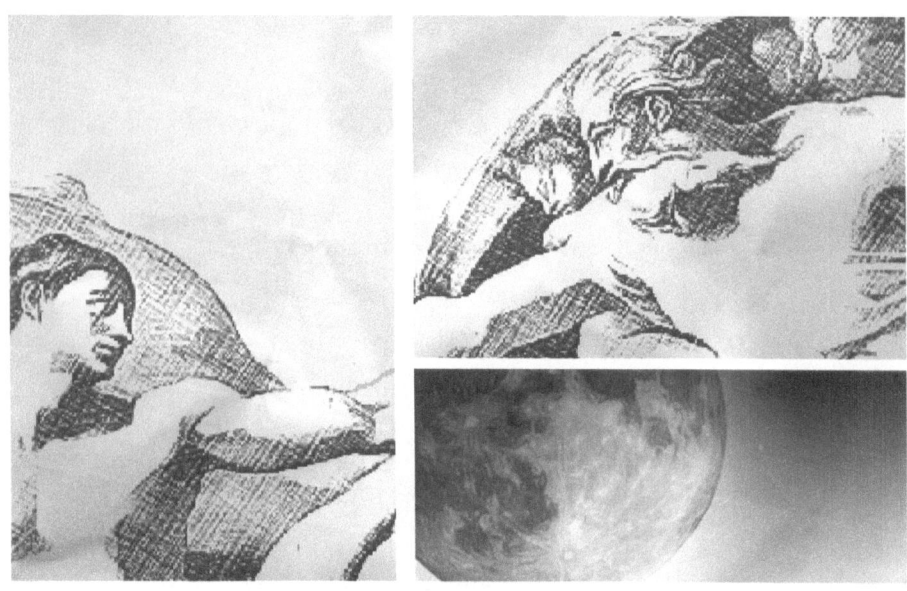

# CEMENT

"I wanted more a time ago, but I was afraid of losing you too. You look beautiful in the moon's glow; the ambiance represents October Blue."

# BUT I THINK A LITTLE LESS

Harvest Moons at 3:41
I am your shadow in absence of the sun
Pour me one, '99 is ever so far
Leave no crumb, profit is you being a star

I stirred shortly then after
Intended to defend you during laughter
Hypocrite I be cause foundation is deep
Tears seeped when I realize I feared society

The bed builds pressure unlearned
I loved you lesser upon my return
Unfair to you when life merely carried on
Building a lifestyle, no time to be a pawn

I yearn your misadventure
I trust your brilliant intuition
I wish for times to treat you better
May you not fall victim to business

# CRIMSON SCARLET

World in hands
Tree of life
Stubborn man
Bloody sight

Weary eyes
Love ungrateful
Be my why
Apple so faithful

More than a day
More than a week
Steady intake
Doctor of sleep

Chip off the block
Nostalgia unmatched
The youth watch
Magenta on black

Shawayne D                                    June 26 2024

# GARDEN SOUL

Sugar water for dreams
Macaroni for the stomach
Coffee pure, filled of steam
This is life on a budget

Accolades for struggle
Ancestral yearn for closure
Truth is the crowd loves you
Lessons learned older

Isolation is an illusion
You are never truly alone
Weapons they're using
I need you to come home

Fear adequately triggered
I cannot outrun my shadow
The garden leaves withered
I welcome the less I know

# A Poem You'll Never Read

And I'm okay with that.
Didn't have to backtrack
Entirely
I've transformed bitter raps

Poetically
The crowd chants my name
The price to stay sane
The outlet to create

The knowledge to be great
This is the last verse.
The illusion of your shadow
Hurts

I'm not the one to question worth
Pain for pain
Abandonment to be free
For the flame, you interrogated the sea

Didn't have to say your name
This is a poem you'll never read

# RESIDUAL

Purple breath epiphany
Debating options carefully
Sun beamed adventures
Ashamed, being self-centred

World bleeds chaos
Prophetic remorse disqualified
Voice beyond course
Unwavering bond advised

Gullible, death not
Miserably, angst rots
Inevitable subtle healing
Love magnificent revealing

# UNDERTAKE

Carrying the weight
Of skeletons
On your conscience
Is no good for the soul

I know of premature goodbyes
The wake of a new day
Ego defeat in the forgiving sigh
Peace is what we create

Heal in your safe space

# GALACTIC

Point me in the right direction
That's the least you can do
Getting lost is my new obsession
I plead loneliness, but ain't no use

Space and time intertwine
Poem remains unspecific
Stars, snow and plum wine
The whole scene is galactic

Tearful eyes as I undertake
Route far beyond the unpaved road
Better must come, role models would say
I internalized that as staying ten toes

# BIEN ADIEU

Soulful interjection
Step into my life
Provoke redirection
I need closure inside

Nerves unsettled
I fear ignorance tainted
Formality levelled
I'm glad that we waited

Why do I care
If the world be unjust?
Looks like I'm here
All alone with all of us

Too much to gain
Too much to lose
I welcome pain
Till we say bien adieu

shawaynD                    June 26 2024

# LAVENDER IN A BOTTLE

Crystallized raindrops pitter-patter
As I sit down to jot, I analyze disaster
More or less capable of dodging obstacles
I clung to labels for lavender in a bottle

Mercy me if there be choice tonight
I have and I will fight for what's right
Perception tainted with a rose hue
Voice aggravated, what did I do to you?

Remedies that make ancestors blush
Doing of my making in a world corrupt
View persecuted for enlightening minds alike
Fear deep rooted however beautiful be life

Gems for the road unpaved
Sage for the lonesome days
Air for the body's functional pleasure
Fire to ignite the joy of us being together

# A Younger Me

Heart on sleeves for the world to see
Focused on illuminating minds with poetry
Body relaxed as slow became the motion
I was better than that, I now step into the open

I blamed the world then you and me
Fought the urge to prematurely leave
Divine timing must interrupt with no delay
I find power in us, here's to a good day

Wicked be karma, I acknowledge their pain
For my momma, feel the grass when it rains
Miles away in a foreign land, I stretch my voice
I remain with scarred hands, leaving a choice

Better be the person, mantel I demonstrate
Depression can worsen, tears on the face
Risen up by beings with hopeful blessings
A younger me seen, I tap into the connection

# UGLY POCKETS

Green into magenta
I still yearn the closure
Pipe dreams to enter
A place of no boulders

I rose above as best as I could
Rooted to a passionate culture
A friend of mine claimed I stood
In a fairytale plagued with vultures

Glitter not be gold I was told
Unfortunate our second meeting
Ten toes be the soul in winters cold
I can tell something darker is creeping

Today there is sleep
No bitterness, victim of logic
I dare you to not settle for defeat
How much you trade for ugly pockets?

# WATTS OF PRESSURE

Raven feathers
Death hath the notion
Times no better
No good with emotion

I wonder still
Of feelings that clung
Were you real
In the place sanity begun

Tender eyes smile
I admire the snow
I'll be here a while
The less you know

Kind-hearted peace
Could I be delusional still?
Haunted by sleep
Ambition can't be killed

# GARDEN HOSE

Sprinkle abundance, it is needed here
Body is able to function, don't feed into fear
Relinquish the thought you aren't meant to be
A contributing member to all of society

I cannot lie yet my heart is pure and true
Better must come, I say to all of you
Rise on up amid shame and apartheid
To speak is dismissed as I'm a good guy

But what is good in the eyes of the provoked?
Shirt soaked after I grabbed the garden hose
I never wanted to remain quiet as it rained
Trauma ever potent so I trade pain for pain

My brother, my sister, my daughter, my son
Hopeful for those around and those to come
Flames of war licking up cradles and rooms
Aquatic blessings calms danger into fumes

# 9AM IN THE 6IX

I said I'd be back sooner than later
But my avoidance didn't do us any favours
You look beautiful as you've always been
Let me see those eyes...the most captivating

Ocean
Devotion
In hoping
Your soul be potent

And willing to step into the open
Your name I carve into the sky
Can I be your why for giving the world a try?
I cannot lie, you feel like home

Expressed in cradling you when we're alone
I need to atone for not picking up the phone
Pride and lust created a rut between us
I hope I'm more than enough

To ignite the hope of sanctification
What we need is glory and patience

ShawnMcD                    June 26 2024

# SAVE THE NOTION

Snow on evergreens
On Halloween eve
I see prophetically
What it cost to be free

Obligations pile on
I wish to stay in the sun
The moon heals partially
Capacity to intensify sea

Stomach on a budget
Greed ain't doing favours
Expectations of the public
Save the notion for later

I am what I am
For now there is now
Believe in a higher stance
Comfort with no ego nor sound

# MINERAL WATER

Versions of you on November eve
I tried grief, simply not for me
"Can't be happy everyday"
That's alright, but today is the day

For a good day, good vibes, good life
I wish for you to fall in love with yourself twice
Along this winding journey, destiny matters not
After you heard of me, you wanted my spot

Hold down the fort and may no force alter
Steady the course with holy mineral water
I care for you still during moments intertwined
Man on the moon of solar systems you find

# HOLD A MEDS

If you know, you know
Shadow boxing with my shadow
Please no photos as I confront ego
Holding a meds in autumn as moon glows

Trying to stay ten toes below elevation
Sitting with self is topic of conversation
I wish to have you with no booze or envy
No rules, resentment of truth nor jealousy

I wish for you to be able to merely relax
Catch a glimpse of beauty like look at that
Ice and fire invoke realization of pure solitude
Could the liars have awfully manipulated you?

# POPCORN CEILING

Anxiety to bring forth a new era
Passion for validation that took care of
Worry running astray on lonesome days
I ain't your enemy, rather a counter part

In the human race
May these words lead you through the dark
Couple dollars for the hopeless heart
That falls hard at first sight and touch

I'm not naive at the world's unfortunate unjust
Just trying to prove I'm enough
I ponder letting you down slow
All that I owe, in the streets with woes

Never lived your life, yet intrigued about mine
Almost everything a sign from the divine
Mercy all my pitiful crimes
What could've or should've happened

Remove the glove and stop capping
It's all love with no iller motive
Channeling my energy to live
Yearn the grass amid the unbothered snow

Lesson learned cause as above so below

# LEFT BEHIND, SHY PORCUPINE

When I moved, you didn't
Come on through, vibe finished
Love or lust, ecstasy enough
World's unjust, no power in us

I let it slide, forgotten grip
Tears in eyes, no better than this
False image, the scene dystopian
Pure wickedness, fondly important

Build you up, to tear you down
Pride and such, closure with no sound
Love defined, beyond lines
Left behind, shy porcupine

Make no sense, make it out the cement
Environment cleansed; heart scrub sufficient
Be free as a chapter, healing over laughter
I own personal disasters, self love comes after

# CIGARETTE SILHOUETTE

Count the sentiments
I need the same type of energy
Blessings for family and friends
There is a protege within me

My inner child wants it pure
A couple M's to stack than count
Give me respect and virtue more
My soul is stuck in the upside down

Admiring cigarette silhouette
You're not the love of my life
I'm not far ahead as of yet
But I'd like to do this all twice

Pain for pain spreads out to a circle
Mirage recognized as ill fitted
Ambition is the game, I'm the colour purple
Your essence and presence gets me lifted

Shannyned  June 26 2024

# BLUMTITE

The saviour never showed
Stuffed my feelings into a 4 door
Weaponized disrespect in my core
Before commencing a mission on Weston Road

Vivid scene for a former timid me
If you're reading this then it be my eulogy
Epiphany of a higher purpose
My haters are part of the circus

Jumping to conclusions
Anger with no true resolution
Laughing along in the face of it all
Uncompromising when I say we ball

Running away from secure foundation
Not exactly the time for conversation
I stepped out with no remorse in my hand
Encountered doubt as you addressed as fham

Being not keen to walk away
Something higher whispered, "Live for today"
Cruising in veins was something rather sinister
Soul waned as the name; I am no better

# TEARS OVERPROOF, A SHOT OF RUM FOR YOU

The need to cry
Entangled with bad days
The art of getting by
Rent needs to get paid

Emotion shrugged off
The inner child silent
For now, we are lost
No need to get violent

I ponder the pain
Pouring liquor calm
True love when it rains
Just survive the storm

Necessary means
Society born anew
Mind and soul freed
I choose to pray for you

# WEIRD AS PER USUAL

The feeling is not mutual
Stop hurting yourself
I'm not quite suitable
Tunnel vision on wealth

Make it make sense
All the stuff I've had to deal
I'm not even from these ends
Your perception of me isn't real

I don't have it figured out
But I'm sure to follow the plan
If moving forward is the chosen route
Then I ask that you leave the upper hand

Dismay isn't cute
Redirect boredom stagnant
Weird per usual are society's feuds
I'm just stuck in my head once again

# FATHER I TRY

I want to see the good
The tears block my vision
Giving into myself as I should
Teaching myself commitment

I want to trade the pain
For understanding true
Belief in a higher power sane
I won't allow them to hurt you

I want to cry momentarily
Due to time being of the essence
Salty, but warm tears flow so free
Do I not deserve worthy connection?

I want the world to witness
Legacy etched into history
May the struggles be dismissed
I am not your consort nor enemy

I want to forgive and forget
For I am merely a human being
Father I try to do my absolute best
A neurodivergent idol publicly seen

# SEASONS AND REASONS

I walk away

Into a pale winter
Childhood dreams
Yearn my arrival back to self
I could have done it for wealth

I walk away

Into the luscious spring
Love born anew brings
Compassion ever so tender
I wish to be here in December

I walk away

Into a potent summer
With memories and euphoria
Passionate energies and connection
I know today is the day wherein I heal

I arrive

Back to a mesmerizing fall
Cotton candy skies, colours and love
Capacity to experience life and then some
I see your pain in the absence of the sun

# *ALL SET*

You're a lesson
Learnt in full
No second guessing
You're reliable

The vision captivates
Timid my ambition
You have always been great
Allow me and the world to witness

Heights reached by you
Amongst the autumn sun
I'm the colour purple
You're lightening in the rum

Out of breath yet peace of mind
The fact we connect is stellar
I reckon you're all set this time
To persevere no matter the weather

Shawayne D                                    June 26 2024

# BOSS REPPING

Alarm set to a quarter to 5
It's 4:30
Sick of the art of getting by
Mercy me

Urgency when the demeanour changes
Life's pages
Seen in a flash as the void's certainty
Weapons anew pointed at me in the spiritual

Price to be free, but the sins are residual
Clenching on the hearts of sons and moms
Moving on while quoting a bit of Psalms
Egotistical of me to relate to being great

Not rich in the physical rather in fate
Connections pitter patter into conundrums
I'm boss repping no matter the bygones

# FOR NOW CONFUSION REIGNS

I trade my pain for your pain
Collecting cents in the cement
Nonsense wherein we lose friends
But you the day 1 after all

Mentality that we finna ball
No matter disasters or disagreements
Silent is the ego and pride is the secret
Living on a budget while dodging set ups

Homie gotta survive so I helped him get up
Hellish memories in vivid description
Therapy ain't enough to allude stress
Fear and everything ugly

For now I ask you to love me
Light years away seemingly
I'm the person you see when you sleep
Everywhere and nowhere at once

Can't even front, they believed I was dunce

# PLATINUM FLOWERS

The vibe I'm on
As immaculate as where I'm from
A land of sentimental nods
Bygones are bygones

When I acknowledge with wagwan
Foundation solidified
I can fly no higher
Run as rivers into tides

The reverend is misunderstood
Compassion reeks
Of vengeance illuminated
Platinum flowers at feet

My dreams have been initiated
Closure good
Enough to dismiss remorse

I hope that you would
Lift me to a higher source

# I Met Her in London

My departure acknowledged like the snow
Stomach full of porridge as I starved ego
Way before decision to come to mountains
I pack bags with love, and I met her in London

I remember the Jack Daniel's mixed with apple
Her team made it to the finals, so she dabbled
The journey didn't matter nor did the universe
Playful banter and captivation by words

Still ain't a proper love poet, but I'm proud
Divine timing shows it, we laughed loud
The repetition left to her coy smirks
I don't know what we're giving, hopefully it works

Perhaps I felt guilty to leave as per routine
Gave her a copy of book 6 from 2018
They don't make that anymore like her laugh in fall
I probably should have asked the score, but would I care at all

# FLATTERED

Thrones of gold and fragile crowns
Intuition bold, the cape is on the ground
Needed be guidance for the hesitation
The violence ain't stranger to conversation

Mortal man I be with heart on sleeve
Urge of philanthropy no matter greed
Society on the verge of a really bad day
Repression of hurt when asked if okay

Jah guidance and praise with potent faith
I can not remain bird in cage, vocation late
Body bruised and battered with obligations
Although I'm flattered, I wrote with dedication

For souls looking for an answer as eyes close
For the beauty in September that joy boasts
For all those who see me as role model true
These words I speak are to inspire all of you

# Fair to Acknowledge

And even if you were to listen
That would be my heart's content
The love I've been giving, leaves me depleted in the end
How must I exhume patience ever less?

You're shining in this room amongst the rest
I'm not where you left me and that's okay
I'm not sure you'd forget me and that's okay
Through the winters cold and summer deeds

I took the unpaved road and you succumbed to the streets

nShawayneD                                    June 26 2004

# COOL AND COLLECTED

The smell of a hazelnut latte
The joy of conversation
The colourful and nostalgic days
You are everything worth waiting

No sly facades
I own shameless rebirth
I shrug the struggle off
I trade diverted eye contact for understanding of hurt

# TURQUOISE SUMMER HUE

Vulnerability
Rocking me steady in the flowing months
I rise towards pinnacles
I break hearts as a philanthropist

I'm not the one for her
I see home as a struggle, but worthy foundation
There are those who love you, no matter the colour of your
patience

# PALM LEAVES AND APOLOGIES

Generational trauma turning on it's heels
Sending blessings to my momma like ain't no big deal
Moved further away from cities of brick
I'm tired right now, but I gotta deal with it

Obligations that don't make sense in the end
Death and taxes skews supportive friends
I understand the upper hand
Couldn't stick the landing so crashed into the sand

Profit is a hell of a thing
Wondering why love for you clings
Disgusted with myself that I can't pull it together
You want to cry, I'm no better.

# TABLE SETTINGS

I am a mess
I am working on love real slow
A partner holds the capacity to redirect
I'm just thankful for another day above ground you know

# THE MARVEL OF IT ALL

Concrete jungle
Stomach rumbled
Leaves you humbled
Please don't stumble

Bitter lies
Pain weaponized
Woeful sigh
I am mortified

Momma Earth
Make it work
Used to search
For hope in church

But I change
You are rain
Can't complain
Times be strange

# COLDNESS CONQUERED

Lower the pessimism
May your happiness not require permission
Moving forward makes all the difference
We're mortals and something pure exist in self image

Aravindo

June 26 2004

# THE SILENT CHOIR

How do I speak on the unspeakable
Doing the best but dragged down by the worst people
Those with ill motives and lack of faith
The room is silent, but the echo is that I was once great

# GLASS HALF FULL

And I dreamt a better hue
The ship steadily rocks
In love with the flow of you
I find myself sitting at the dock

# OPINIONATED

This is a beautiful moment
All things considered
I'm healthy
My friends good
Talent runs through
The world still needs healing
I suppose everything is everything
The mortal coil be temporary
My seed will live on
Something higher leads me forth and I am not scared

# DILIGENCE

Pure joy rids discomfort unpleasantly
For us all to make it is what I want to see
Reminder that the path is uncertain
Every step forward means the universe is working

# UNDISPUTED EMPATHY

I feel the thunderous beat
The Glorious Rhythm
Before I could speak
Emotions gathered a million

Short notice on arrival
What more to alter
Leave the car idling
I can not be the mentor

Victim to devious plots
I see more passionate hues
The weight on shoulders is a lot
I pray for all of you

# FLOWERS FOR AMBITION

Where's the disconnect?
Am I human enough to command respect?
I stand beyond ignorance
I trade my knowledge for your two cents

Pity me not
Just awoke so I jot
With soulful emotions
Leaving you be represents devotion

Internalization that I'm the bad guy somewhere
Unlike my past life, this time I persevere
My idols fall like flies, flowers for ambition
May hope not die and we proclaim significance

June 27 2024

# HELD LIKE COCO

Can't make everybody happy
I missed you before you were gone
All I got is this poetry
Outlet for causally moving on

# FLOODLIGHT

"Humbled by life's page, but I'm not bird in a cage."

# ABUNDANCE REGARDED

Mountain air in my lungs
Heart beating like a drum
Fresh kicks on my feet
Hair nappy since prime begun

Lots of love to give unconditionally
I envied others healing before looking within
My capacity to live, create and let free
The image in the mirror is not the opposition

I feel what you feel in the lonely sense
Here to rise you up further and more
My dreams bore through the cement
I heard the rose is nimble without thorns

Siding with grace formed as a divine presence
I hated myself until I stumbled upon you
What we learn from departure is I'm a friend
May you build a future of dreams anew

I can't fathom the journey nor read minds
I'm not eager to step behind the veil
When I see you I'm reminded of sunshine
Illumination of waters waiting to be sailed

# BODY

To feel your love
As I have
And have not as of yet
I sacrifice breath and self respect

This scene isn't for the timid souls
I don't want you partially, I want you whole
The ground is the divine ancestor
The sun will never love you lesser

And if woes interfere enviously
I will shelter you ten-toes with my body

# THE BLARE OF THE VOID

Nightly runs split into intervals
Still in the streets with my woes
All that I was told coming back up
About to vomit the fear of being stopped

Before reaching the pinnacle
Deep down I'm utterly miserable
That she'll leave me in her wake
I think intensity of the passion I create

To see is a blessing unmatched and untainted
Perhaps this be truer than what's conversed
My mirror's reflection is stuck in hurt
What is my worth?

# BEIGE BRICK COUNTERFEIT

Casting paranoia into the abyss
What you mean it doesn't get better than this?
Beige brick counterfeit, merely wanted a home
It's no game nor trick, reality being I'm alone

Lord of the land provokes head in hands
Hoped you'd understand that I be mortal man
With aspirations, next up is another generation
Conversations regarding endless payments

It may be greed, struggle or higher intellect
There is a need to come collect the check
Inbound are charges for air and movement
Stay woke while deliberating common sense

Shawayne D                                    June 27 2024

# ALMOST SETTLED

Not really sure or whatnot
Eager to pour without rocks
Stressed a lot, but you mighty fine
This is Hennessy, not your typical wine

Thanks to the divine the morning after
Drinking your smile and soaking your laughter
May the universe bless you
Can't believe I almost settled

This ain't a poem about how I resent
You left my heart damaged on the cement
But so it goes, I'm still dodging photos
And associates that are loco

Figment of a future that never existed
The proof is that without you I'm feeling terrific

# FOR WORST RATHER THAN BETTER

Sent you well wishes
You held a dagger to my throat
After coming back from fishing
Boat nearly capsized

But this ain't the day you die
I'd rather you baptize the ego
The ganja will numb you slow
Pride is timid and body nimble

I stumbled into dark rooms of gold
Disturbing imagination for a 3-year-old
All that's bound and certain to come
There's a hold in your bottle of rum

Heaven announces entrance with drums
Foreign still believed to be a land in the sky
For worst rather than better be the notion
This ain't the day you die my friend

Instead you face your darkest demons
As sins wash off into a bloody ocean

# LIFE BE LIFING

Peace onto you, love note to society
May challenges be few, this is in fact reality
Blood stains reflective of destructive harm
Endless pain when a loved one dies in arms

I swallow concepts of the heart of people
Silver tongue, no bullet yet utterly lethal
I heal when you do in the pouring rain
I reckon rent is due cause I saw your pain

Doctors illuminating matters of hereditary
Fuming and willing to resort to necessary
Means convened in basements and tents
Refried beans and toast was sufficient

Highs into lows as the sky is blue sometimes
I despise the mistletoe held by lovers of mine
Winter cycles in which I can't move from bed
Life be lifing, but maybe that too is in my head

# AND I STILL SEE YOUR PAIN

Nothing less than peculiar be the situation
Wants and needs analyzed in conversation
History in the making as people come together
I see you as a counterpart in society

Let us heal together
I wish you better with words sweet as apple pie
Compassion forever as you keep getting by
Dodging premature demise taunting around

A single tear from my eyes as I fell to the ground
A community rises up the worthy soul
May this be my values when I grow old
Rejuvenating the mind by not lying that I'm fine

Sitting wholeheartedly with myself before the grind
Be not still, weather the storm that wails
It's okay to feel, repression isn't the best meal
Media drains, problems provoke, envied name

Flowers blooming and I still see your pain

# Humble Growth

Skyscrapers are the office view
After putting in labour I come home to you
My love sublime in a tender hue
I believe in humankind, the glory we can do

Not too fazed as I once was
Don't need material wealth, may I have a hug?
I'll give so as long as you don't shove
I know this be the virtue of powers above

I heal in the safe place of protecting my heart
We'll meet at the end of light meeting dark
Problems lessen and dreams become ideal
Compromise the depression and finally feel

Growth of humility instilled long ago
Silence lives in the void of the ego
I'm supposedly defined by what's surrounding
This a rhetorical reminder to a future me

Capacity for my love not to be meek
May divinity flow throughout vicariously
Strength in friends, family and those weak
A brother from the ends with dreams to speak

# Mindful Manners

Sentimental nod
I think it's a good day
Hope can not be robbed
There's a need to elevate

You are my brother
You are my sister
Humanity beyond dollars
Well wishes I send you

Continued disregard
Of grim reaper's taunts
Why is everything so hard
Is it a sin to simply want

Flowers for the journey
I'm not giving up just yet
Florescent uncertainty
That I must suffer unvexed

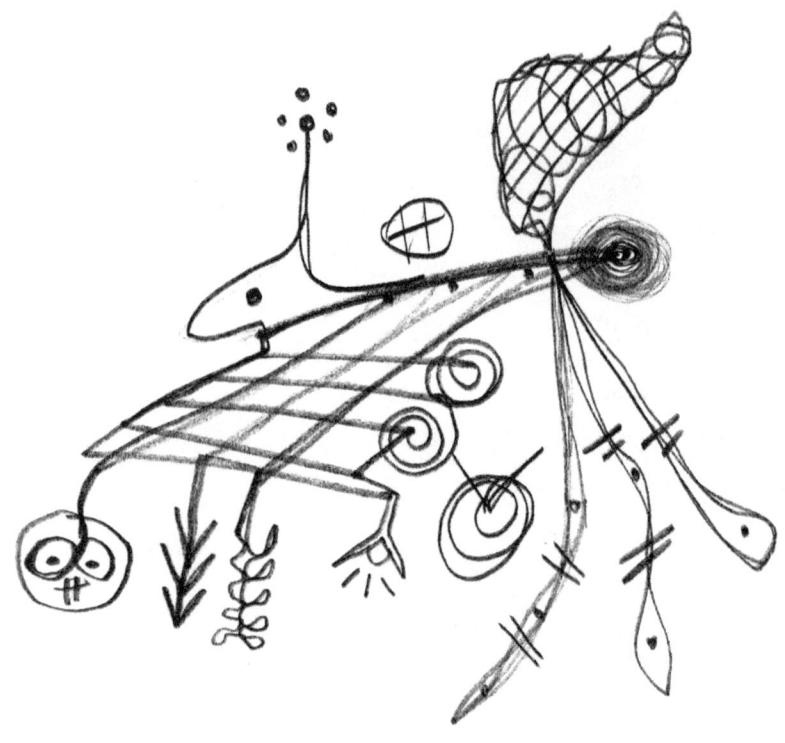

'Shawayne'                    June 27 2024

# STUPENDOUS

My world swooned beneath a blue moon
Please come back, but not too soon
Peace of mind comforting in your absence
I hope to find you amongst this room

Worthy be this moment after all this time
The music is melancholy paired with wine
Shimmering as you did so long ago
This is youthful lust and maturity combined

Be no stranger, I've grown as I should
No sense on paper, but I bet I could
Interject the norm of walking past
Chances of you staying is no good

That's okay and rather how cookie crumbles
Horizon called out over whisper of a mumble
I paused between half goodbye and new hello
My conscience sighed and stomach rumbled

Possibility of coincidence for me to finally listen
Cotton Candy Skies, but something's missing
Disrupted stride, you found an old flame
Can't withstand the weight of failed commitment

# To Sit with Oneself

I've started to fall in love with life again
Not too sure when I fell out of love, but I know
There are things I'd like to stick around for
You looked beautiful this morning

Tears for acknowledgment, admiration resides
I hope to find home in those eyes when I'm 63
I'm in a tug of war with the ugly sides of me
Paired with an uncertain society, I'm 6ft deep

Please see that I too deserve compassion
Lust sneers it's face then and again
But I know you're worth fighting for
These moments refine like wine with age

I'm the space bound poet
But you aren't a damsel in distress
A queen with ideals and means tenderly so
I heal slow with a messy heart

Abundance of time in lieu of the dime
Let me hear your story ambitiously true

# THAT'S TUFF

I understand that I could never understand
Empathetic, but I'm not a better man
With head in hands I undertake a plan
To deliver you from mirages of sand

They want dreams weaponized
And youthful innocence to take backseat
I thought all of us crossed t's and dot i's
Where is the brotherhood that you speak?

I know not what is certain
Especially to a lesser degree
The attacks aren't working
Still healthy and keen to see

What a beautiful world with abundance
They lack vision in the grips of drama
I see your pain and conclude that's tuff fham
Lessons inherited from fathers and mommas

# HERO SLIDE

All that talk, but when I arrive y'all moonwalk
Out the scene, skin pristine, invincible to envy
Black excellence waiting for money at the dock
I am who I am, I attract the most unseen a lot

Weird is normality in failure to plan
I'm a hypocrite diabolically meek
I can not morally outreach my hand
For the sins are an ocean and I drown deep

Words like pencil to pad, I spit the flow reckless
Similes like Tetris, interference is a death wish
Old school meets new school in broad day
Don't be stingy with the food or ending in GTA

Never had to touch road with laces undone
Said he was your bro, but homies can front
No first name basis, but business far from last
Honorary cases that completely collapsed

# JUKE HEAVEN

I carry legitimate virtue
May these words hurt you
Pour my vices stronger
I need my money longer

Disorientated ego in tow
I want to watch it burn slow
Cursed melodic, but prideful ambitions
May the fear suffocate and know submission

Can't walk the other side in a white suit
Without coming to realize I ain't bulletproof
Hunger on my mind, force combines
To feast in decadent eyes, I am wine

But the heart knows no mercy
The soul's fate is filled of uncertainty
Pocket of dimes as I approached the reverend
"May you age in time, but not juke heaven"

# THE HERMIT'S SHELL

No more will I fall victim
You can keep that energy
Something better I'll become
As I choose myself and leave

Four walls, I'm the loneliest soul
Ambition calls from no caller ids
I want it all as long as it's owed
Usually the advocate of peace

Battered and bruised I say kindly to you
There would be no nectar without roots
Pain comprehension remains oddly mute
Guilty by association interwoven by group

Writing this on a whim, I need more closure
Archetype in everyone's eyes, love a better me
Truth was I couldn't sing; I grew much bolder
If I fail to internalize demise, let applause free

Destination fallacy undoubtedly so
I wept some tears that cold November
One morning gratitude sung gospel notes
If you're reading this, know you're remembered

vShawyneD                    June 27 2024

# ASKING TOO MUCH... I RECKON

The dysfunctional heart is no bueno
I fall apart before we start because of ego
The ships have sailed, and I'm stuck on land
Well of purity depleted, please understand

They want me to suffer and then some
I'm sorry dawg, too far I have come
From the mud, concrete and necessary means
Y'all deserve hugs, there's meaning in dreams

Still don't got it figured out as I wished
Took the unpaved route by topping my old shit
When will satisfaction sneer it's ugly face
Easy to be depressed, hard to be great

Winging this as best I can with fear in hands
Don't kill the vibe of divine timing and plans
May the new day teach me peaceful lessons
Simply asking too much...I reckon

Storms in eyes, I weather your storm
Merciless pouring, part of healing's importance
I'm still giving life a chance everyday as I can
Agony in strife interpret joy as contraband

# ASH IN THE CUP

Supposedly I'm blessed
Supposedly I should be less stressed
Supposedly happiness for a check
Supposedly in love with sides I hope you forget

I ain't too sanctified to choose higher ground
Waiting on my downfall, look at you now
Ain't blood rather love on crisp evening snow
Lord above laughter infiltrates false shadows

I'm fighting back even though life is a trap
A struggle embarked mission with no map
How you take my words like gum in broad day
You inherit the hurt before bitterness sprayed

This for my day 1s harbouring demons
I remember not seeing the sun, I need to heal
The smoke and liquid confidence ain't a secret
Is me wishing you better a part of the deal?

# STARFRUIT INTERLUDE

Losing people more than a few
I am sorry for whatever I did to you
Could it be—I'm still assuming again
No point in this, you're no longer my friend

The emotions swallow me whole and bleak
Stormy days, fiend-full pleasure, I don't speak
I analyze pitiless lies belonging to my soul
I've been on the run for some time, time to go

No place like home, but she yearns distance
If I wasn't so miserable, I could learn bliss
Same routine, highs into lows, I sloom dire
Not gold that gleams, I cry slow, honestly tired

I'm bothering you with lonesome suggestions
Beautiful words cut through transgression
Take me for something yet leave no bruise
Everything is nothing, this is starfruit interlude

# Pardon The Mess

Stress can be self destructive
Lows deepest when I feel everything tenfold
Intervals of pardoned interruption
I can't keep self sabotaging as I aim for goals

I should do better, the world still needs healing
I should do better, this poem is truly revealing
Repetition irresistible to the pretentious mind
Free me from darkness by giving love ever kind

Today is the eve of something rather grim
If you only knew the topic spoken was sin
Heritage kinda scary, but the blacker the berry
Stainable conscience, I fear being on the fence

Valley to the sea, thirst for validation, holy debt
Patience paper thin, I need to win, self respect
Where do these plans lead and why can't I cry
If in that moment inquiries leave, I would fly

It's not healthy to avoid and call it all noise
Unsteady be the road, but accurate is voice
I dream a better dream wherein I tell the rest
Vision blurry and energy low, pardon the mess

# IF WE THINK ABOUT IT LESS

Figment of my lonesome imagination
Today is the anniversary of deprivation
Mind needs sense and I got 18 reasons
Abundance of friends throughout the seasons

I try my best to keep my word
I tried to explain it in the latest book
Going against the assumptions heard
I can't wait for all of you to take a look

Never will measure up to what came before
Word play immaculate as the passion in core
I analyze the flawed mentality in ambition
A tad bit more of anxiety it's honestly giving

Hallways into homes, please answer phone
Experience foggy, I heard a voice in the lobby
Gratitude evermore, bitter death, love held me
Worth fighting for, more than less, I'm pleased

Shadow of mine in world learning to be kind
Soul assigned to bring forth change divine
If you heard, you heard, if you know, you know
Dopamine's elaborate surge, The Truman Show

# 8:19

No need to sugarcoat
I got the memo loud and clear
My world is falling apart
And you simply don't care

1 in a billion
Yet assumptions of the ego
High as the ceiling
Gentrification walking in stilettos

Shawayne D                                    June 27 2024

# 18 Cents

A dime
A nickel
3 pennies
Equates to
18 cents
At least I'm not
Late on rent
The struggle is the rose
That grows in cement
The struggle is feeling
Like I'm alone once again
I needed those items I put down
Fear in my body as I navigate around
Boulders as I grow older
Life is the ultimate joker
Lessons appear to push further
I'm 18 cents away from a burger

# FOCUS MORE

Anxiety grabs the reigns
How much it cost to feel my pain?
I'm ashamed that I'm a vegetable
No cause to feel this miserable

Surface level disregard
Pass a drink in lieu of scars
I'm merely hoping to give a lot
Compassion frees us from this spot

What is done must be appreciated
Another day gifted; another day created
To capture the dream hidden behind doors
My heart desires gleam, I need to focus more

# IGNITION TO SPARK

Shadows of my past self
I'm a person that needs potential
Generational trauma into wealth
Not sure the world will be sentimental

Tears the size of raindrops mid autumn
I slunk deeper into a paranoid craze
Problems are inevitable as we got them
I see epiphanies in your tender wake

Retribution in mind, rest the nimble body
They spoke of the cost of crimes
Invoked due pleasing being a hobby
Somewhere you lost me there and everywhere

The joy closure brings is everything
I need to win
As deep be the ocean
As sweet as carelessly hoping

I relinquish the thought of misguidance
Tell shyness to slender back to the dark
Majestic start with ignition to spark

# TAKE ME AS I AM,
# WHATEVER I AM

I figured what I felt was all in my head
I am proud that I stayed true and overcame
Lately it's been hard to rise from bed
Lately it's been hard to remain the same

Abundant mind creating scenarios array
I second the thought that it will get better
I like it dark along with the interwoven day
I don't really mind the cold so have my sweater

I'm a better me in the future somewhere
I shutter at my struggles in the present
What I've learned from the past is that I care
Shelter me close, if not I'll learn a lesson

Blessing be ability to breathe long and deep
Cracks in the facade of heavenly vision
What if I said that she spoke rather sweet
Personification of the human condition

# RUTHLESS REPERTOIRE

Kindness didn't work
Hope on the back burner
Self reflection in church
Glory never heard of

Promiscuous rhythm
Virtuous soul and remarks
Doing well with life given
Shed some light in your heart

Notion of eye for an eye
The daily struggle amid woes
Today is not the day I die
I've chosen to remain ten toes

Deep in the concrete jungle
I made it to evergreens and orange skies
Ambition disregards the thought to be humble
I deserve better as I keep on getting by

Surge of the alter ego
I know the power of greed and quickness
The mortal coil isn't just for show
It is capable of destruction and wickedness

# WEATHER THE PAIN

I couldn't stand the rain
I couldn't stand the snow
Glorious skies finally came
Illusion of mind fitted aglow

Patience embedded within
Heart skips a needed beat
Light isn't the opposition
Allow inner child to speak

Messy environment noticed
This second I sit with myself
Discovering emotions important
Love capable of invoking wealth

I need all my people to win
You smiled beautifully today
Weather the pain undertaken
We can be the change made

# PASSIONFLOWER

I got trauma
You got trauma
Crying mommas
Nights so somber

Slippery slope
Murder you wrote
Passionate smoke
How you finna cope

I hope in intervals
Most are miserable
The anger be subliminal
Definition in the residual

Details torn out
Purity over clout
Pessimistic doubts
Full bloom in a drought

# UNTITLED

I can't find a name
I gotta pay my dues
Long path to fame
Peace be with you

Only blood within
May tears shed slow
The opposition is grim
Reap all that you sow

Not at the pinnacle
Yet far from the abyss
Pride seems cynical
I pray I grow from it

Conquer the despair
Present at the door
Painful stories I share
Illuminate shame at 24

The day is close yet so far
Hanging on the word maybe
During the silence I'm a star
In your memory I find safety

# TRIFECTA OF STRUGGLE

Not enough time, money or love
Infatuated with signs, honey and hugs
Peculiar it be that we haven't made it yet
May I inform the creator that I can't accept

Bitter dues formed this half-hearted interlude
I care for you, but the struggle is me and news
Perception of misdirection invading dire mind
Judge not my complexion when chaos unbinds

Worth the find during expedition of guidance
If I cross that line, I'll live in void of your silence
The violence perpetrated against one another
Far from greatness, but we certainly do better

I won't lecture for long as I do in the book
Perhaps this is a song when you take a look
Bars for bars, eye for eye, just trying to get by
Lonesome hours, crying skies, struggle inside

# Purposeful

The pain is residual
May hope intervene tenfold
I try my best to be sentimental
But life be lifing so you how it goes

Miraculous it be
The possibility to succeed
Odds stacked against we
Uncertainty within society

No more bitter judgment
On my sleeve I wear forgiveness
Not personal yet done with logic
Vertical be the road to eternal profit

Jotting this effortlessly with no flow
I hope tomorrow illuminates you purposeful
Material items, but in the end they can't go
Foundation cemented invincible to obstacles

I look towards my photogenic generation
A group that hide sorrows from conversation
Therapy, overdue healing and spiritual highs
The truth that I see is that self pity forever lies

# Lunch Run '16

Polished shoes drill concrete
The hunt for food to fuel dexterity
I got like two dollars to my name today
That's alright I'll just wish the pain away

Stomach rumbling for something sufficient
It's either a Timmy's thing or local business
Food will prove enough even for the youth
Breaking some rules yet adventure we choose

A Thursday evening some months later
I held a potluck filled with love and laughter
I just wanted to prove caring was important
Struck a nerve so voted as valedictorian

Years after yet I still send sentiments
Back to day 1 friends from ascension
Those in the community still doing their thing
Remember when our biggest worry was wings

# BITTER BLUEGRASS

Few poems away from conclusion
October blue discovered after illusion
I undertake the task of creating before I pass
Onlookers may laugh, that's bitter bluegrass

I'm writing this close to a quarter century
In the future I hope there's a happier me
If you're reading this there's a chance to heal
Current times proves moving forward is a skill

I never imagined making it this far
Walking in the night I'm a star
Motivating with dreams I create
I must mention that everything's at stake

The lesser the haters the more of stagnation
This isn't a jab rather an overdue conversation
I ain't no saint, but I hold the faith to a degree
Streets wet with paint as we pray patiently

Written on a whim, I know something is coming
For future children, may fear you not stomach
Embrace the passion present from the get-go
I'll be holding on till the day you say let go

# LENIENCE

Manic phase finished
For seemingly a moment
I resent my self image
That's my greatest opponent

I can't keep lying
That I'm fine and all
Ego slowly dying
Inner child gently calls

I need to take care better
Can't pour from empty bucket
Feeling under the weather
No money trees in the budget

Nourishment of time
In which I see all the flaws
May I age fine like wine
Rebuttal of sorrowful clause

Treat me with compassion
With a sprinkle of love decent
May these poems be everlasting
The profit I crave is lenience

# A PRIDEFUL BLUE

Concrete jungle
Traded for mountains
I'd say I'm rather humble
But I wouldn't mind abundance

Severed relations
I need to focus on me
Remorseful locations
I think it's time to leave

Written this be
A week before Tumblebug
October blue adds to the legacy
Allow me to show you all love

Forms of gratitude
I philanthropy weak
I believe in each of you
Be the change that you seek

Rather hopeful in this second
One day you'll hold this in hands
A couple months only I reckon
In the meantime, please understand

# OCEAN TO DOCK

Weighted I stand
Beneath the upper hand
Kindness seemingly reprimanded
High as the universe till I landed

Lessons scar the miserable thought
Hope be not lost when virtue the cost
Stand amid the rubble with no profit
Colder be the huddle so I code switch

Nonsense to waste all the time
Lessen the friends, embrace the mind
May you discover peace rather than silence
If I choose to speak, will I fall victim to violence?

Societal norm to pain alone
Microphone marries metronome
Prolific surge of energy to the dome
Be at peace whenever you roam

# HIDDEN CORE MEMORY

I care too much.
Just enough to stuff woes deep below
You look like sunshine after wind blows
Might as well depart from dire mentality

In the mirrors reflection I no longer see enemy
I'm grateful for those who rise me like rose
Jungles of concrete was all I used to know
I cried, I fought ego, I gave the day a try

Love sighs, vulnerability shows, am I bad guy?
I'm running from things I don't remember
Uncertain about whether you'll read this by October
Sense of closure knowing I left an impact
Stuck between a boulder, but I can't backtrack

# VERANDA ON PORTOBELLO ROAD

Was there ever a doubt
For us to finally make it out
Of the ignorance and jealousy

That breathes retaliation if disrespect speaks
The exchange for success is to worry less
I'm just happy that for now my people blessed

Writing this during a passage of passion
Plotting dreams and mapping further wins
My emotions take hold sometimes, human condition

The heart speaks bold if I take time to listen
The energy morphs, fluctuates and flows
Got birds in kitchen while I drink a Negroni outside Veranda
on Portobello Road

# AMONGST IT ALL

All the things I never said flow like water
In this moment
I see your capacity to covet eternally rather than temporary
Eclipse of the soul, I pray my dreams don't fold
I walk with eyes closed into rooms of gold
No mark of the beast, I need rum after such speech
Audacity to plot harsh encounters, my heart breaks
How much must I take before I leave legacy in this place
Front and centre I am, with body bruised
This the end of October blue
A love letter to those curious after the fall
Please know I found hope amongst it all

# THE BLUNT OF IT

Murky waters calling out to me
May friends not turn a blind eye
If I'm to go far with this poetry
The hidden aggression has got to die

Black boy fly in a pale blue hue
Perhaps you'll find your why some time soon
I elaborate with heavy heart in this moment
The plot was devastating, I see you as the opponent

I yearn peace of mind and comedic relief
Suffered defeat before I had a chance to speak
There's no honour amongst thieves
Comprehension elite, do you breathe slow in repeat?

# For the Sake of It

Prime suspect of living on a budget
Halfway between church and "run it"
Excuse the aggression, but I meant what I said
Days above ground a blessing, stress in head

But the bills be true just like taxes too
What we finna do if pain catches attitude
Leaving hope bruised and us questioning use
Of further movement beyond the cement

I'm affluent in friends, the love sometimes ends
Lesson learnt like getting burned, never again
Fearful of capacity in lack, I try to pull life back
On deathbed can't backtrack, dreams to stack

Visions of a future wherein others uplift
Doing due diligence as I spread this gift
You may laugh, cry or even find it amusing
Reality is that struggle makes us all human

# BLOOD MOON IN A CLOUDED ROOM

Ripped the image out the mirror
Just to analyze a bit clearer
I found one of stature and composure
Notable laughter when I describe boulder

On chest, but I could never love you less
Change might detest persistence reckless
Makes perfect sense, stack and give thanks
This room may dank, but minds put together make bank

I feel it slow, pain inevitable like sun rising daily
The need to know, left miserable with maybe
The world doesn't burn amid the chaotic state
Compassion earned as you willfully appreciate

Mortal traits to investigate greater fate
Such a path doesn't mean invincible to aches
Especially those to the heart and beneath soul
Face to face with competition of same mould

# WATERMELON RADISH

Green into white, white into red
Starry night with aurora overhead
I count my blessings while admiring view
Upon self reflection this is a moment for few

I see riptides in eyes that aren't mine
Justified astonishment awoken with time
I feared the animosity would cling ever so deep
Beauty in the rose that grew from concrete

Hungry mind for pleasure to mortal coil
I feed the thought after laying in soil
Proof a brighter future henceforth
I bow my head and say a prayer to Lord

I seek understanding for pain
I hope to live up to the mantle of last name
I'm eager to make those around feel good
I'm here to make amends for all I should

The sky is a phoenix blooming in the wind
May we come together for a time and soak in
Love, admiration and thoughts of being better
Watermelon radish hue is the current weather

# Henceforth

I call back my power.

Riptides in eyes, but I'm no longer somber
Contemplation of tribulations in October
They want to tear me down on path unpaved
I'm deaf to the nonsense while hoping to get paid

Love is rage.

I'm not keen to open slightly
The pessimism been haunting low-key
The cost to be free is heart on sleeves in night
I'm not the abundance you need, but I figure you'll be alright

Give me fortune.

Teach me further what's important
Regardless if falsehoods illuminated is notion
Ambitious as it gets wherein I fall into more
I should get a bit of rest just to settle the score

I am human.

# APOLLONIAN

May enlightenment accommodate
Humility from way back then
Soul ties penetrate guilt-stricken face
In this moment I'm your friend

To build a home, I sever the past
Am I alone in getting what I've asked
Respect with diligence of tomorrow being fair
Compassion despite ignorance of me in clear

I'm reluctant to dismiss ambition
The vibes immaculate when I ponder
Give me more and may it reflect commitment
My hands are sore, but I will hold on longer

Discipline and gratitude in perfect dance
Your energy lifts me high with no fear to land
Ripped from the past like Doc in DeLorean
I holster the mask and pursue pure Apollonian

# POETRY AND POSTCARDS

More or less
I lean from stress and heartache
Bitterness tasted traded for honey full interval
I can not be miserable at the thought of your absence

Boy to man
I question lifespan when world goes belly-side
In you I confide, no tears in eyes to degree
Education on elevation, poetic soliloquy

The path unpaved
I lean from wicked ways internalized by fear
Being loved is capacity in which we persevere
Sorrowful days put on pause with you here

Profound attributes
Being the proof of all to come
The reflective image prompts me not to run
Finding balance in world as sky has spun

I should address you by name
Pondering if the affection is the same
We know struggle so the norm is to work hard
I hope I don't bug you with poetry and postcards

# JUGGERNAUT

I move forward valiantly
Thank you all for rocking with me
Every follower, every soul, every friend
It was a pleasure to bestow book 10

Long way since 2016 and confusion
Now I am seen with these words I'm using
The love will come if it's not already here
Capacity of a thousand suns, but I stand with no fear

My brother warned me in a past life
"Be still and virtuous yet don't fall victim to the night"
I sat and prayed after I rinsed my feet
This is praise to a higher power we can't see

# ACKNOWLEDGEMENT

Today was a sunny June Day

The year is 2024 and I'm currently 24

I never expected to make it this far

10 books in 8 years, I'm flabbergasted

I would like to thank Hunain Jawed for illustrating the cover of October Blue

I dedicate this book to an old friend

I welcome hope because fear ends

You wouldn't believe the time we're living in

Be the spark, listen to your heart and may your light never dim

# AUTHOR'S BIO

Shawayne Dunstan is a local author and artist living in Banff, Alberta. He has written 10 poetry books. His artist and brand name is Shaweezy which represents seeing the lights in the darkness. He is a graduate of Humber College. October Blue is Shawayne's 10th addition to his saga. This collection is dedicated to healing, gratitude and being a role model. With grace and love, Shawayne elaborates on struggles, triumph, and self-acceptance. The author recognizes challenges in this ever changing world before asking the reader, "Why not bet on yourself when you know you better than anyone else?".

www.ingramcontent.com/pod-product-compliance
Lightning Source LLC
Chambersburg PA
CBHW050846150626
46549CB00012B/160